UNIFIED DISCOURSE ANALYSIS

Discourse analysis is becoming increasingly "multi-modal", concerned primarily with the interplay of language, image, and sound. Video games allow humans to create, live in, and have conversations with new multi-modal worlds.

In this ground-breaking new book, best-selling author and experienced gamer James Paul Gee sets out a new theory and method of discourse analysis which applies to language, the real world, science, and video games. Rather than analyzing the language of video games, this book uses discourse analysis to study games as communicational forms. Gee argues that language, science, games, and everyday life are deeply related and each is a series of conversations. Discourse analysis should not be just about language, but about human interactions with the world, with games, and with each other, interactions that make meaning and sustain lives amid risk and complexity.

Written in a highly accessible style and drawing on a wide range of video games from *World of Warcraft* and *Chibi-Robo* to *Tetris*, this engaging book is essential reading for students and researchers in discourse analysis, new media, and digital culture.

James Paul Gee is the Mary Lou Fulton Presidential Professor of Literacy Studies at Arizona State University. He is author of many titles including *An Introduction to Discourse Analysis*, 4th edition (2014), *How to Do Discourse Analysis*, 2nd edition (2014), *Language and Learning in the Digital Age* (2011) and co-editor of *The Routledge Handbook of Discourse Analysis* (2012).

UNIFIED DISCOURSE ANALYSIS

Language, reality, virtual worlds, and video games

James Paul Gee

Routledge
Taylor & Francis Group

LONDON AND NEW YORK

First published 2015
by Routledge
2 Park Square, Milton Park, Abingdon, Oxon OX14 4RN

and by Routledge
711 Third Avenue, New York, NY 10017

Routledge is an imprint of the Taylor & Francis Group, an informa business

© 2015 James Paul Gee

British Library Cataloguing in Publication Data
A catalogue record for this book is available from the British Library

Library of Congress Cataloging in Publication Data
Gee, James Paul.
Unified discourse analysis: language, reality, virtual worlds, and video games / James Paul Gee.
pages cm
1. Discourse analysis – Psychological aspects. 2. Video games – Psychological aspects. 3. Computer games – Psychological aspects. I. Title.
P302.8.G44 2014
401'.41 – dc23
2014000281

ISBN: 978-1-138-77451-3 (hbk)
ISBN: 978-1-138-77452-0 (pbk)
ISBN: 978-1-315-77445-9 (ebk)

Typeset in Bembo
by Taylor & Francis Books

To Bead

CONTENTS

LIST OF FIGURES

1

INTRODUCTION

Hundreds of thousands of books are published each year just in the United States. Many more are published each year across the world. It is hard to come up with a topic that has not already been written about a great deal. For better or worse, you are about to embark on reading a book that is about something that has, as far as I know, never been written about before. This is so, in part, because this book seeks to unify topics that are of interest to quite different people and quite different fields of inquiry.

This book is about discourse analysis, language, meaning, video games, the real world, imaginary worlds, human development, and life. Discourse analysis is a rather sleepy field in linguistics that analyzes language as it is used in specific contexts. It is not a field that gamers have shown much interest in and discourse analysts have shown little interest in video games, though there is an emerging interest in multi-modality (words, images, and sounds mixed together). People have, of course, studied how language is used in games, but they have not used discourse analysis to study games themselves as communicational forms.

This book is an exploration of whether we can create a new type of discourse analysis. It will explore whether there can be a unified theory and method of discourse analysis that studies language, games, science, and human action and interaction in the real world and in imaginary worlds. This theory and method will treat human language as foundationally connected to conversation. It will treat conversation as a turn-taking form of interaction that humans can have with each other, with the real world, with other worlds, and with video games. And it will treat humans as themselves complex worlds.

Why feature video games in the mix? Because video games are a new form of media that allows humans to create, live in, and have conversations with new worlds. They can illuminate the nature of conversation itself and allow us to bridge between language and the real world as scientists study it and as we all live in it.

Video games will allow us to see that an expanded notion of discourse as the study of an expanded notion of conversation can connect discourse not just to language and worlds, but to human development, the structure of society, and the nature of human life.

Now I must admit that we cannot know (yet) whether this enterprise—this enterprise of attempting a unified theory and method of discourse analysis of language, games, and worlds as deeply related things—is possible. We cannot know until we try and we cannot know our first try has worked or not until others chip in (or not). Perhaps the task is folly. But at least it is new.

Why even try? I am now an old academic (65 as I write this). I have come to believe that too much of academics has too little impact on the world. I have come to believe that too much of academics is too narrow and too often separates things that belong together. For me, science is a human collaborative enterprise based on respect for the world. Today, as we humans have brought the world to the brink of crisis by how little respect we have paid to it—to the environment, to global poverty and inequality, to ideologies run amok—we need to realize that respect for "reality", for the world, is fundamental to being human and indeed for survival.

I want to argue that language, science, games, and everyday life, for all of us, are deeply related and each is a series of conversations in which we can flourish only if we proactively find a good alignment between who we are as individuals and the various social, cultural, natural, and imaginative worlds in which we live and seek meaning. Discourse analysis should be about life. It cannot answer the age-old question about the meaning of life. But it can show us how we humans go about giving meaning to life.

I will argue that thinking about language can illuminate how we think about video games. I will argue that video games can illuminate how we think about language. And I will argue that both language and games can illuminate how we think about and live in the world, actually in multiple worlds, including worlds we create.

It may well be that readers interested in one topic here will have little interest in the others, despite the fact that I am arguing that all the topics in this book belong together and are, at a deep level, quite similar. However, as a discourse analyst, gamer, and human being I find these three identities deeply complementary. I hope I can convince you that you yourself are all three of these things and that they belong together. I will succeed here, even if the larger project fails, if I have engaged you in a good conversation.

Keep in mind that this book is not definitive, but tentative. It is not an end, but a beginning. It covers a few landmarks in a possible new terrain, not anything like the whole territory. It puts some marks on a map, but the map is incomplete. Nonetheless, I want to suggest that discourse analysis could become an integrative science of meaning making in human lives and society. I want to suggest that discourse analysis should not be just about language, but about human interactions with the world, with games, and with each other, interactions that make meaning and sustain lives amid risk and complexity. Video games, the world, and language will all be on a par here.

Those who do not play video games may see them as ephemeral and much less significant than language. And in one sense they are. They are a very new form, much newer than literary and far newer than oral language. We are concerned here more with their potential than their current reality. They are a new form of world making and problem solving.

Those who play video games may see language and linguistics as boring and irrelevant to games. But games, I will argue, are a type of language and language is a type of game (really a set of games). They have much to teach each other, especially about what it means to think, imagine, act, play, work, and live.

The terms I use in this book will often be old ones used in new ways, words like "avatar", "conversation", and "worlds". And, then, there are those troublesome words "real" and "reality", contested terms indeed. The "real world" is available to us only via interpretations and different worlds become available through different interpretations and different tools (e.g., a microscope).

Nonetheless, the world we interpret "talks back". Our tools and interpretations lead us to act in and on the world in different ways and the world answers back, we get a result. Of course, we have to interpret this result as well, often as good or bad for our goals. But the world can very much bite back and hard if we ignore it or disrespect it. There are plenty of dead or sick people—maybe now the whole of human society—that have learned that the world does not put up with just any interpretation, use, or abuse.

This book argues that we humans have consequential conversations with the real world. Such conversations are the basis of science and of a sane and humane life and society. As with our fellow humans, we need to talk to the world with respect and care. If, in the end, you do not think the real word is real in the sense that it has its own ways and can bite back, I don't recommend telling it so. Lately the real world seems a bit grumpy, what with all the human caused and human denied global warming, toxic spills, and species extinction and all.

This is an academic work, but I have tried to write it for a wide audience in the sense that it covers topics of interest to a diverse array of people and fields. Since we are exploring a new field—one that may or may not actually come to exist—we have to sometimes stretch the meanings of words and play with ideas in new ways. I have tried to express my ideas in several different ways so that they might become as clear as possible, at the risk, though, of repetition.

People who are not gamers will not necessarily know about the games I discuss and that is fine. I have tried to make my points about games clear even for non-gamers. Gamers will not necessarily find the language data I discuss familiar, but that is fine as well. I hope they will see how language used in the world to do things is a lot like playing games. I hope, too, that gamers and language people alike will see that science shares a form of life with the work and play that all of us everyday people engage in all the time in order to survive and hopefully flourish in life and in games.

I have written about discourse analysis (e.g., Gee 2011, 2014a, 2014b) and I have written about video games (e.g., Gee 2004, 2007, 2014c). But I have not heretofore brought them together. I have, over the last decade, dealt with audiences in the two areas quite separately and they have rarely mixed. However, I have long sensed that there is a deep connection between the two, but only lately have been able to explicate that connection in words. The words are in this book. The connection has changed my view of language and of games. I hope it does yours as well.

Notes

Now, all of the above is not meant to say that there is not much important and highly relevant previous work in both games studies and discourse analysis. So, let me say something about the literature in both these areas.

Game design and game studies

For those not familiar with games, game design, or game studies, I would highly recommend starting with Raph Koster's *A Theory of Fun for Game Design* (Scottsdale, AZ: Paraglyph, 2004). The book has line drawings accompanying the text. It is written by a well-known game designer and is both entertaining and savvy.

If readers want to delve more deeply into game design, here are three outstanding books: Tracy Fullerton, *Game Design Workshop: A Playcentric Approach to Creating Innovative Games* (Burlington, MA: Elsevier, 2008); Jesse Schell, *The Art of Game Design: A Book of Lenses* (Burlington, MA: Elsevier, 2008); and Katie Salen and Eric Zimmerman, *Rules of Play: Game Design Fundamentals* (Cambridge, MA: MIT Press, 2004). Greg Costikyan's *Uncertainty in Games* (Cambridge, MA: MIT Press, 2013) takes up themes that importantly supplement my discussion in this book. Mary Flanagan's *Critical Play: Radical Game Design* (Cambridge, MA: MIT Press) takes things deliciously further. Anna Anthropy's amazing book *Rise of the Videogame Zinesters: How Freaks, Normals, Amateurs, Artists, Dreamers, Drop-outs, Queers, Housewives, and People Like You Are Taking Back an Art Form* (New York: Seven Stories Press, 2012) shows how in gaming and game design to let everyone in.

For games studies, I would start with Jesper Juul's *Half-Real: Between Real Rules and Imaginary Worlds* (Cambridge, MA: MIT Press, 2005), a book very relevant to my discussion in this book. His other books, *A Casual Revolution: Reinventing Video Games and their Players* (Cambridge, MA: MIT Press, 2012) and *The Art of Failure: An Essay on the Pain of Playing Video Games* (Cambridge, MA: MIT Press, 2012) are well worth reading too. See also Simon Egenfeldt-Nielsen, Jonas Heide Smith, & Susana Pajares Tosca's *Understanding Video Games: The Essential Introduction* (New York: Routledge, 2012) for another fine way to begin.

At a more technical level, Ian Bogost's books *Persuasive Games: The Expressive Power of Videogames* (Cambridge, MA: MIT Press, 2007) and *How to Do Things with Games* (Minneapolis, MN: University of Minnesota Press, 2011) are combinations of game studies, rhetoric, and philosophy and they are highly relevant to my discussion. Mark J. P. Wolf's *Building Imaginary Worlds: The Theory and History of Subcreation* (New York: Routledge, 2012) is highly relevant as well and his two theory readers, *The Video Game Theory Reader* (New York: Routledge, 2003) and *The Video Games Theory Reader 2* (New York: Routledge, 2009), are important collections. Jon Petersen's fascinating book, *Playing at the World: A History of Simulating Wars, People, and Fantastic Adventures from Chess to Role-Playing Games* (San Diego: Unreason Press, 2012) is important background for some of the issues in this book. Christopher Paul's *Word Play and the Discourse of Video Games: Analyzing Words, Design, and Play* (New York: Routledge, 2012) is the best and most accessible combination of games studies, rhetoric, and discourse studies to date. If my book bores you, read his.

Discourse analysis

There are innumerable books on discourse analysis. The best book to start with is, in my view, Ron Scollon and Suzanne Scollon's brilliant *Narrative, Literacy, and Face in Interethnic Communication* (New York: Praeger, 1981). Then read everything Ron Scollon ever wrote. I am prejudiced enough to recommend also starting with either of my books: *An Introduction to Discourse Analysis* (London: Routledge, 4th edn, 2014) or *How to Do Discourse Analysis* (London: Routledge, 2nd edn, 2014). For those who do not trust authors recommending themselves (and why, indeed, should you?), start with Rodney Jones' wonderful book, *Discourse Analysis: A Resource Book for Students* (London: Routledge, 2012). Follow up with Rodney Jones and Sigrid Norris, *Discourse in Action: Introducing Mediated Discourse Analysis* (New York: Taylor & Francis, 2005), a book quite relevant to the book you are about to read. Teun A. van Dijk's *Discourse Studies: A Multidisciplinary Introduction* (London: Sage, 2012) is a good collection of articles. Another good way to start or continue: Norman Fairclough's, *Analysing Discourse* (London: Routledge, 2003), followed by anything else he has written (and he has written a good deal).

All of the above works are not cited in the text below, but all serve as essential background for myself as writer and you as readers of this book.

A note on citations

This book develops in a new direction views I have long worked on in the areas of discourse analysis, language, learning, and games. That work is covered in Gee (2004; 2007, org. 2003; 2011, org. 1996; 2014a, org. 1999; 2014b, org. 2010). These works have appeared in new editions and they cite the literature behind my views for those who want to pursue the literature further. In a great many cases in this book I am discussing my own viewpoints on issues about which not much has yet been written. My remarks on games, in particular, are based on my own game play and participation in the gamer world. That said, as my comments above show, much relevant literature has indeed appeared. Finally, let's be clear that I am by no means arguing in this book that my approach to games or to discourse analysis is uniquely right or worthy. Each is but one approach to its domain, good for some things and not others.

2

CONVERSATIONS

Language, worlds, and games

Meaning

We are all comfortable with the idea that words have "meaning". But what does it mean to "have a meaning"? Words and phrases mean things to us because we are familiar with social conventions in terms of which a word like "puppy" in English means YOUNG DOG and "large mouse" means a MOUSE THAT IS LARGE FOR A MOUSE. Meaning is simply a matter of social conventions just like a strike in baseball is. "Three strikes and you are out" is a "rule"—a convention—in baseball. That "puppy" means YOUNG DOG is a convention in English.

Human languages are communication systems that rely on shared conventions about what words will mean (Gee 2011, 2014a). There are other sorts of communication systems built on conventions but ones which do not use (or do not only use) verbal words and phrases. Mathematics is one such communication system. It is clear that we give and get meaning from mathematical symbols much as we do with language.

Conversation

Oral language is not just a set of conventions for how to mean with words. It is also a tool for having conversations. Conversation is a turn-taking system. When we speak we design what we say in anticipation of a response. When we get a response, we design what we say next with due regard for the response we just got. Our listeners do the same as they engage with us. We each take our turns. We each shape what we say based on the responses we seek, anticipate, or actually get. In the end, conversation in language is co-constructed, co-designed, and performed collaboratively. Conversation is the product of "us", not just "I" as an isolated individual. It is like a dance.

Linguists and sociologists have argued that face-to-face conversation is the primordial and most fundamental form of language for humans (Sidnell & Stivers 2013). We use language in a great many other ways, but human conversation is what shaped language from its beginning. In fact, face-to-face conversation with adults is crucial for a child's development, socialization, and later success in school and society.

Unlike speech, writing ("literacy") is not good for conversational turn taking. Writing is responsive in the sense that writers must anticipate and hope to shape the reader's response. But writers do not and cannot respond back to the reader's response while the reader is reading. Letters are a form of conversation, but they are slow and they seriously constrain the range of responses that can be displayed.

Well, this was all true for most of the history of writing. But, perhaps, not anymore. Text messaging and some other forms of social media are quick turn-taking systems. In text messaging, we anticipate, shape, and respond to responses and, in the act, together co-shape, co-design, co-construct what we say. Text messaging is a form of writing that is a bit like speech. Nonetheless, until text messaging allows for more ways to show emotion, the range of responses will remain more restricted than in the case of face-to-face conversation.

For most of their histories, film, books, and music have not been turn-taking forms. Films, books, and music do not respond turn by turn to the viewer, reader, or listener and thereby co-shape an act of continuous meaning making. Viewers, readers, and listeners can respond in their minds—or to their friends—but their response cannot change the film, book, or music. Books, film, and music are not reciprocal or co-designed. The "author" is all important.

There are forms of improvisational music and theater and we could imagine digital improvisational books. But these are not pure turn-taking forms. In pure turn-taking forms the responder (listener, viewer, or reader) gets to take a turn at production. In conversation, I speak (produce), you listen (consume) and then you speak (produce) and I listen (consume).

Turn-taking systems make us take the risk that while we start out as the boss—the original speaker, designer, producer—we end up, at best, as a co-participant and even at times a bit player in a play we started, but which the inmates have taken over. Sometimes this is the most liberating outcome for speakers and designers. Other times, it is not so good for them. But it is a risk they always take.

Conversations with the world

Intriguingly there is one turn-taking system that is older and even more primordial than verbal conversation. Even many sorts of animals can engage in this turn-taking system. This is "conversation with the world" through actions and not words.

And there is one radically new turn-taking system: video games. However, radically new as video games are, compared to language, they nonetheless take a ride on the nature of our ancient conversations with the world, as we will now see. Video games essentially create new worlds to have conversations with, worlds designed by humans.

What is a "conversation with the world"? We humans have long engaged with a cycle of thinking and action that is essential to our very survival (Gee 2013). This cycle goes this way: We want to accomplish something. We form a goal. Then we act. Our action can be looked at as a probe of the world, a sort of question we put to the world. The world responds to our action. The world's response might indicate that our action was effective as a way to our goal or it might indicate that it was not. We reflect on the world's response and then we either reconsider our goal or act again in an attempt to elicit further responses from the world that will allow us eventually to accomplish our goal.

This cycle is simple: form goal—act/probe—get response from world—reflect—act again with due regard for the world's response. We and the world take turns. We repeat the cycle until we succeed or until we see we cannot succeed, in which case we get another goal.

People who do not pay serious attention to responses from the world that tell them their actions are not working well, put themselves at high risk for failure and even at risk of harm and death. Of course, sadly, we humans today often do not listen to the world. For example, the world has been telling us, in response to our actions, that it is getting too hot. Yet we do not change our course of action. This is as disrespectful to the world as it would be to a conversational partner. If we conversed with people this way, we would alienate them and come to regret their responses. The same is true of the world.

Humans (and some other animals, like the primates) developed, in the course of evolution, a souped-up and super-sized version of the conversation with the world. They developed the ability to simulate and role play in their minds so they did not have to act too soon in the world or with too much risk. Humans can imagine what might happen before they act. They can role play other people and even things to imagine how things might go. They can think before they leap.

We humans can imagine what might happen if we ask someone out on a date in a certain way, say by trying to use humor. We can even role play other people and seek to imagine how they feel, what things look like from their perspective, and what they might do. This is the foundation of empathy. Humans can even imagine being things like a hunting wolf or, as Einstein did, a light beam. When we imagine what might happen we use our former experiences as a basis to make predictions.

This ability to simulate, imagine, and role play in our minds greatly enhances our conversations with the world (and, indeed, with other people). We can form a goal, run a simulation/role playing session in our minds, decide on an action based on how things went in our simulation/role playing session, pay attention to the world's response, reflect and perhaps even do another simulation/role playing session, and act again. This allows us to lower risk and to make much more powerful hypotheses or guesses about what we should do.

The human power to simulate and role play in our heads is the basis of consciousness (Hood 2012; Kahneman 2011). It is also the basis of our human sociality, since we humans can imagine things from the perspective of others (thanks, in part, to mirror neurons). What we do in our heads is more than a simulation. It is much more like a video game (Gee 2004, 2013). We design a world in our heads, based on our past experiences, and "play" ourselves and/or other people. We humans appear to have evolved long ago the capacity to "mod" experiences and to "game" experience in our heads. ("Mod" is a gamer term that means "modify" and names the activity where gamers use the software by which a game was made to modify it or transform it.)

The human conversation with the world—super-sized through our mental powers of modding experience in our heads—is basic to human thinking and survival. We use it in our everyday lives all the time, whether we are gardening, driving, cooking, or mating. In a more formal version—and a version super-sized yet further by new tools and technologies—it is the basis of all science.

Science is a high-powered, tool-enhanced, socially and institutionally organized conversation with the world based on respect for the world's responses. Scientists use simulations they can build on computers, not just ones they can run in their heads. But their computer simulations usually do not allow them to "be" the electron, the light beam, or the wolf pack's leader. The scientist watches the simulation from the outside, so to speak, from a god-like viewpoint. The scientist does not act within the simulation as a part of it, as we humans do in our heads.

Nonetheless, scientists often and readily talk and imagine as if they were indeed what they are studying. They use their mental video game design capacity—enhanced by the experiences of the world they have had as scientists—to imagine being an electron, a light beam, or a member of a wolf pack. They can see and "feel" the world from the perspective of an electron, a light beam, or a wolf. They can also imaginatively enter their graphs and simulations and act things out in their minds.

Video games as conversations

Turning now from the very old—our capacity to carry on super-sized conversations with the world—to the very new, we come to video games. Humans have invented only one truly new—radically new—turn-taking form beyond our conversations with the world and with each other in language. This new form is video games.

Video games are a truly new form of turn-taking conversation. And in historical terms, they were invented yesterday. Yet, new as video games are as a technology, we have just seen that humans have long been able to run video games in their heads. Video games as a technology just externalize our human capacity to mod and play in our heads. In this sense, video games take a free ride on a mental capacity—simulation and role playing—that we humans have long had.

Think what players do when they play a video game (Gee 2004, 2007, 2014c). They treat the game as a world and they probe it and reflect on its responses in hopes of accomplishing their goals. While playing, they build their own simulations/role playing sessions in their heads of what might happen in the game world if they take certain actions, make certain decisions, or engage in certain strategies. They can even imagine being one of the NPCs (Non-Playing Characters) in the game or one of the other human players in a multi-player game. They are "modding" the game in their minds. They are building a model of the game and game world in their heads and testing it out before they act. This is just model-based reasoning (the core form of advanced science).

We humans were all modders (transforming the world in our heads and in reality) before we were game designers and we players are all modders in our heads when we play intelligently. A video game is a piece of the mind made public in the world of things. When we play video games we confront the nature of our own minds. A video game gives us a new world to probe and with which to have a conversation. And, perhaps, these new conversations can teach us things about the real world, about language and learning, and about ourselves and our minds.

When they carry on conversations with the world, some people believe they are having conversations with a designer, with God. But, in reality, the world was not designed, but evolved. The world is vastly more complex than any game world. That the world is so complex is the reason that scientists often study models of parts of the world and not the world directly. Nonetheless, games are often complex enough that players have to build models of the game and its rules system in their heads and reflect on how the rules might work to help them accomplish their goals. We usually do not play games just by mashing buttons with no thought and reflection (though we can if we like).

Games are new. Oral language is at least 50,000 years old, maybe much older. Written language is much newer, at best 8,000 years old. Video games are only decades old. They are baby forms of communication. So, we do not know yet how far they can go.

There is a long academic history of analyzing language. We have a good many different academic disciplines devoted to analyzing oral language (e.g., linguistics, discourse analysis, philology, phonetics, and conversational analysis, etc.) and others devoted to analyzing written language (e.g., literary criticism, rhetoric, stylistics, and hermeneutics, etc.). We do not have any discipline analyzing video games as an interactive communicational form, because video games are new and we do not yet agree how and even whether they communicate.

Here is my argument: Video games do communicate. Furthermore, they are a turn-taking form. The player acts and the game responds. They involve a turn-taking, real-time, responsive and reciprocal conversation. Therefore, they are potentially important for human communication. I say "potentially" because they are new and we have explored only a very tiny bit of their potential.

Since video games involve an interactive (turn-taking, responsive, reciprocal) conversation, they are, perhaps, open to analysis as a conversational, discursive form of communication and collaborative meaning making. We can, perhaps, develop a communicational analysis—or what linguists call a "discourse analysis"—for video games, alongside what we already have for oral language. Of course, in gaming we are having a conversation via meaningful actions and not just via words. But we have seen that we have conversations via actions with the world in everyday life and in science.

Perhaps, we can discover something yet deeper. Perhaps, the analysis of video games can illuminate, change, and transform our analysis of language. In turn, perhaps, our analyses of language can illuminate video games and the contributions they can make to culture, society, and communication. In any case, we don't know until we try, though, of course, success is not guaranteed.

I have distinguished between conversations with other humans via words and conversations via actions with the world. But I would argue that these two types of conversations are not as different as they may at first seem. In conversation we use language to engage in actions, actions like promising, supporting, questioning, encouraging, threatening, and many others. We predict what response we will get from our listener when we speak and we reflect on the actual response we get in formulating how we will proceed toward accomplishing our goals. We treat the other person as a world to probe and act on and with. Language is a form of action and people are complex worlds, as we will see as this book proceeds.

Problems

In trying to explore whether there could be a field devoted to video games as a communicational media, let alone one unified with the analysis of language, we face a problem immediately. In fields like literary criticism and film criticism, many of the texts or films being studied tend to stay around and be readily available. Video games go out of date quickly. As technologies change, older games come to look old and become unplayable on modern equipment. While classic books and films still get read and watched years after they were produced, classic games are not often played, save perhaps on emulators or older pieces of equipment. As anyone who has written about video games knows, mentioning games in a book means that soon the book itself will sound out of date as new games come out and old ones get played less and less.

Then there is another problem. Games are fast changing. As technologies change, games sometimes blur into other forms like simulations, digital stories, and even movies. It is hard to predict how games will develop (and what we will call them). Many new forms will surely arise.

And, too, as far as I am concerned, there is no one general category of video games all of which share some essential set of features. Rather, there are many different types of video games. "Video game" is a "family resemblance" concept. This means video games share some rough similarities, different similarities with different other games, and not identities—just like members of a family.

Since games are variable and changing, all we can do is analyze some paradigm cases in the hope of developing principles that apply somewhat widely, though not necessarily to everything called a game or related to one. After all, part of the excitement here is to map out not just realities (what already exists) but to map out possibilities (what could exist) as well. We can discover not only what has been done, but also how designers might create something new by varying from what has been done.

Now we face a final hard problem. Oral conversations, films, and books all have content. We can converse about cats, weather, or politics. We can have a book or film about war, crime, or baseball. Video games, of course, if they have stories, appear to be about something and, therefore, to have content. But, then, not all video games have stories. Even when a game does have a story, it is not clear that its story is all that the game is "about".

A game like *Tetris* simply involves manipulating falling blocks. There is no story. So if it is a conversation between a player and the game, what is the conversation about? The various *Call of Duty* games have stories, but aren't they as much or more about what the player does than the game story the player has not him or herself written? Content is a vexed category for video games.

Let's talk first about games that have stories, like *Call of Duty* or *BioShock*. Such games have stories in several different senses or ways. There is the top-down, author-written story that the player did not write. This is the sort of story books and films have. Then there is the story of the player's moves, decisions, strategies, successes and failures, and what the player has learned and accomplished in the game. This is a story the player creates through decisions, reflection, and play. It is the narrative of the player's course of play.

We all realize that it is inherent in video games that the top-down story, if there is one, must leave room for the player's decisions and actions to matter. The reflections and decisions a reader makes while reading a book make no difference to the book. But a game must somehow change and respond to player's decisions and actions.

In games, the top-down story usually exists to help shape the player's story and the player's story is predominant. Recently, some games have become so much like movies or digital stories, that the player's story—the player's decisions and actions—seem to exist just to allow the game story to unfold and to recruit the player's attention and engagement with the story. Indeed, some games now come with a story mode where "players" can basically just watch the action.

This new trend—part of the convergence of games and movies—raises anew the issue of difficulty in games. Games, for many players, are not games if they are not challenging (although there can be debate about how challenging they ought to be and how much they should or should not cater to different levels of players). Games where players' actions seem to be there only to drive the story forward are often not very challenging. Or, at least, we can say that a high level of difficulty will mean many players may not see the end of the "movie" (and story).

A game series that is a good example of where the player's decisions and actions are subordinated to an authored story is the *Walking Dead* series of games. Players make decisions and the game adapts to them—so we do have a conversation. But the decisions and actions are really in the service of making the story unfold and getting the player to care about it. This series of games is quite good. It is an example of where video games and digital storytelling are beginning to converge. Indeed, we could imagine a future in which television shows work like the *Walking Dead* with viewers making and debating decisions. Nonetheless, *Walking Dead* is not very challenging as a video game (and it is not meant to be), though it does encourage thought and reflection.

So we will see, in any analysis of video games as conversations, we have to deal with the question about the role of challenge and difficulty in games. Gamers are used to the fact that in traditional relatively hard games, they have to "earn" the ending of the story. They do not see the ending unless they have put up with the difficulty of getting there. But this is not now true of many games and will be even less true in many cases in the future.

I will argue that questions like this one—about the role of difficulty in games—and many others have to do with what type of conversation a game is setting up. There are different types of conversations in both oral language and in games. Some are more challenging than others and each type has a different purpose and different sources of enjoyment (or tension).

So, we can say that games with stories are about two things. They have "content" in two different ways. They are about the top-down story. This is just the sort of content books and films have. They are also about the player's story—the tale the player can tell about the flow of decisions, reflections, responses, and outcomes that the conversation between game and player has triggered. This is content in a new and different sense. We can always ask about the balance and relationship between these two stories in a story-driven game.

In a game without a story—like *Tetris*—we have as content only the player's story. In these cases, the player's only story is the story of the player's confrontation with problem solving and his or her own identity as a learner and as an engager with problems and patterns. Such learning and engagement is for many of us a great deal of fun. And, indeed, we will have to explore why so many people find this sort of enterprise so much fun.

However, games like *Tetris* seem trivial to some people, just a matter of time wasting activity. Indeed, all games seem this way to some people. Nonetheless, when we get to why humans find things like *Tetris* so absorbing and so much fun, we will see that the sort of fun and engagement such games offer is not trivial at all. This sort of engagement and fun is at the very heart of science and of being human. It is exercise of a very real human "super power", a power that today is being taken away from many human beings, though it is part of our human birthright. This is the power to gain a sense of agency and control by insight, effort, and pattern recognition.

Summary

To summarize: I am using the word "conversation" to mean a turn-taking exchange in which each turn anticipates a response and, after the initial turn, is shaped by previous responses. I have delineated three types of conversations: conversations in language between or among people; conversation with the world either in everyday life or in science; and conversations between a player and a video game.

I have argued that long ago humans evolved the capacity to play video games in their heads. They can imagine and act as themselves or other people or things in their heads and not just in the world. Video games externalize this mental capacity and, in that sense, are models of the human mind.

Games have content in two ways. One way is the same way books and films do, a story designed by someone else. The other way is the record (and memory and recall) of the player's own decisions, actions, and responses to the game. Some games have stories in the first sense and some do not. All games have stories in the second sense. Our conversations with other people and with the world have stories in the second sense as well.

We will be seeking to develop a "unified theory" of conversational communication, a theory that covers verbal conversations, conversations with the world (in everyday life and in science), and with game worlds. In the end, I will argue, as well, that our unified theory will also help illuminate non-conversational types of communication, forms which have evolved from or after conversation.

3

AVATARS AND AFFORDANCES

Aesthetically driven vs. goal-driven processing

Let's consider two ways humans can process the world. One way is aesthetically. Here we revel in details without pushing ourselves to accomplish any very specific goal beyond enjoyment or appreciation. This is how we look at paintings or read poetry when we take them as art. We can also look at the everyday world this way if we choose.

The other way of processing the world is more specifically goal-driven. Here we look just for what we need to accomplish a specific goal. We look past any details that are irrelevant to our goal. This is how we usually look at a map or read a technical manual.

Of course, we have goals when we engage with art. However, these goals are more general and diffuse than when we are more specifically and strictly goal-driven. When we engage in aesthetic appreciation we may have such goals as enjoyment, spiritual enlightenment, consciousness raising, or the development of new insights. But when we engage in what I am calling goal-driven processing of the world, we have more concrete goals like getting plants to grow in a garden, confirming a hypothesis in science, beating a boss in a video game, or convincing a colleague to vote our way in a committee meeting.

Usually when we read a poem or a literary novel we are more aesthetically driven—paying deep and wide attention—than we are when we read information texts. When we read the latter, we are usually goal-driven and look for specific things, tuning out material that is not relevant to our purposes.

Being goal-driven can cause us to miss a lot, maybe even miss things that might have been more important or relevant than we had thought. So it is good sometimes to surface for air and ask if we are missing the forest for the trees. But, on the other hand, people who are rarely goal-driven don't accomplish much and they can't play most video games or engage in most science, both of which demand that we accomplish specific goals. Now, of course, there is, in reality, a continuum here. There are mixtures and matches, in between cases, between purely aesthetically driven and purely goal-driven processing.

One in between case is one I will call "goal-driven with an eye for surprise". These are cases—common in video games and in innovative sorts of science—where we are goal-driven, but also on the look-out for the unexpected, for innovation, for an emergent possibility that can make us see things in a way. This can be a "have your cake and eat it too" way of being in the world. We can accomplish goals but still appreciate the beauty and unexpected possibilities of our game, text, or science.

Affordances and effective abilities

When we look at the world in a goal-driven way we actively seek for *affordances* in the world. Affordances are what things are good for, based on what a user can do with them (Gibson 1979). For us humans, a hammer is good for pounding nails. That is one of its affordances. A hammer is also pretty good at being a paper-weight or a murder weapon. These are others of its affordances. It is very bad at being a toy for infants and you simply cannot use it as food. These are not affordances of a hammer for humans.

Affordances are only affordances, though, given that a potential user of the object has the ability to use the object to carry out the action it affords. The user must have what we can call an *effective ability*, the ability to effect (carry out) the affordance. Humans usually have the effective ability to use hammers for pounding nails. Animals without an opposable thumb do not. They cannot properly hold the hammer. For us humans, hammers do not have an affordance as food. But if they have wooden handles, they do have such an affordance for termites. Termites have the effective ability to eat wood. We humans do not.

Human life and survival is all about finding affordances which one has the effective abilities to put to good use. Let's say you want to get across a creek. You look around. The log on the ground would afford you the opportunity to cross the creek if you have the ability to move it and good enough balance to walk across it. A line of rocks across the creek would afford you the opportunity to cross the creek, as well, provided you have the ability to walk on wet and perhaps slippery rocks. The creek affords you the opportunity to cross it by swimming across if you can swim across a fast-moving current. Your burly friend could get you across by carrying you if you can convince him to do so and you are able to put up with the humiliation of being carried across like a child.

We look at the world around us to find things with affordances that match our abilities so we can accomplish our goals. Let's call this process of seeking to align or pair affordances with effective abilities the process of "aligning with the world". People (and other animals) who are poor at aligning with the world risk danger, failure, and death.

Fundamentally, dealing with the world, playing video games, reading texts, talking to people, and doing science all involve finding and using affordance-effective ability pairings. They involve successfully aligning ourselves with the world. Even in aesthetic appreciation there are aspects of paintings, for example, that are affordances for a viewer's aesthetic pleasure only if the viewer has the ability to see them or see them in the right way. If you are color blind, for instance, you lack the effective ability to use colors of certain sorts in paintings for aesthetic appreciation.

When we are goal-driven with an eye for surprise, we seek to discover new, innovative, or hidden affordances or effective abilities. Who would have thought that birds could be good at delivering messages (i.e., pigeons) or that scientists would learn to put viruses into bodies in order to cure diseases and not cause them?

Avatars

Video games with avatars (playable characters) are special and very interesting in terms of affordances. Just as we humans do in the real world, avatars in video games have their own distinctive effective abilities that determine what are and are not affordances for them in the game world. For example, a deer in *World of Warcraft* affords the opportunity for skinning to get leather only to playable characters who have the skinning skill in the game. Players choose skills for their characters or avatars and if they have not chosen the skinning skill, then a deer does not offer the affordance for skinning for this character.

Thus, in a game with an avatar, a player does not seek to align with the game world—to find affordances which he or she has the effective abilities to use—directly, but through the avatar. If the avatar just comes with certain set abilities, then players must live with these. Sometimes, though, players can choose abilities or develop them for their avatars. In this case, the player can choose to some extent how the avatar will align with the world and, thus, too, how the player will align with the game world as well (through controlling the avatar).

Avatars mediate our alignment with the world in a video game. It is important then to understand what an avatar is. An avatar is actually three different things. First, it is a *surrogate body* for the player in the game world. Different avatars can and cannot do different sorts of things well and this helps determine what the player can do in the game.

Solid Snake in *Metal Gear Solid* can sneak, make stealth kills, and sense danger. Ryu Hayabusa in *Ninja Gaiden* is a ninja who can leap off of walls, jump across wide gaps, and engage in expert martial arts moves. Chibi-Robo in *Chibi-Robo* is a four-inch house-cleaning robot who can helicopter across small gaps, clean surfaces, and climb chests of drawers. The avatar determines what physical actions a player can do in a game. The avatar determines the affordances for actions in the game and the effective abilities the player must have or gain.

The avatar as a surrogate body also determines what and how the player can see and sense in the game world. Some avatars can see through walls with a sort of

X-ray vision. Some have devices that can map out the best routes to take through the game world. Some can move noiselessly and fade into shadows. Obviously what and how the player can see and sense—determined as it is by the affordances of the avatar—becomes in turn opportunities and constraints the player must live with and work within.

An avatar is not just a surrogate body replete with powers and limitations. An avatar is also an *identity* that a player inhabits. This identity is determined by the game's story. So Solid Snake is a biologically enhanced rogue warrior saving the world from hidden conspiracies. Gordon Freeman in *Half-Life* is a scientist seeking to escape from and possibly stem an alien invasion. Chibi-Robo is a four-inch robot who cleans house and tends to the happiness of the family members in the house. Lara Croft in *Tomb Raider* is the daughter of a rich English family and an intrepid global explorer. The stories in these games tell us who our avatar is, what they should be able to do and how well they should be able to do it, and why they want to or have to do it.

When we play a game, we play as the avatar. We enact the identity of Solid Snake, Gordon Freeman, Chibi-Robo, or Lara Croft. We do not just inherit their ways of acting and seeing, we inherit who they are. Often gamers try to pull off actions and accomplishments in a game in the spirit of the avatar. If I have played a boss battle poorly, I may play it again, even if I have won, to be sure I have lived up to the sort of hero Solid Snake is supposed to be, the expert marshal artist Ryu Hayabusa is supposed to be, or the courageous explorer Lara Croft is supposed to be. Indeed, in some cases, players cannot succeed without living up to the standards tied to the identity of the avatar (the first *Ninja Gaiden* game is a good example; the game is quite hard and demands a certain level of mastery appropriate to a master ninja).

Another way—less common, but important—to look at an avatar is as a *tool-kit*. The avatar, in terms of his or her skills, powers, and devices, offers the player a set of tools with which to accomplish goals and solve problems in the game.

Solid Snake, as I said earlier, can sneak, kill quietly, and hide very well. He has a radar and communicational devices with which he can map out routes, anticipate enemies, and make plans and strategies. He can manipulate a little robot that can enter and see into spaces he cannot. In many war games—like *Call of Duty*—the avatar can use high-tech weapons, command other troops, call in air strikes or artillery strikes, and use night goggles. On the other hand, in the beginning of the first *Half-Life* Gordon Freeman, fleeing an alien invasion unleashed in an underground lab, famously has only a crow-bar and no real battle skills.

The avatar determines many or all of the tools a player can use. Here, by tools, I mean the skills, abilities, powers, and possibilities the avatar offers to the player as ways to accomplish goals and solve problems. I mean, as well, the tools and technologies an avatar has available and can use. For example, in *Deus Ex* your avatar has devices to hack computers, pick locks, and augment his body with cyber powers of various sorts. In *Sly Fox*, Sly has a great many gadgets that can accomplish all sorts of things as Sly and his team engage in *Mission Impossible* sorts of plots.

So an avatar is a surrogate body, an identity, and a tool-kit all at once. We players confront the game world and look for ways to accomplish goals and solve problems through the avatar as body, identity, and tool-kit. We align with the game world not directly, but via the possible ways the avatar can align with the game world. We seek for affordances that match our effective abilities not directly, but via the affordances and effective abilities open to the avatar.

Solid Snake is good at stealth. He is the sort of character who looks for affordances in the world (e.g., hiding places, shadows, and hidden air ducts) where he can put his effective abilities for stealth and hiding to good use. Thus, too, the player must do the same. If the player is good at playing a stealth game, then Snake and the player are a good "team".

Solid Snake can fight and shoot, though this is a less effective way to play the game. This can become an inferior way to play the game for a player who can play shooters well but not stealth games well. The player is using Solid Snake against his grain so to speak. In the *Thief* games, the lead character, Garrett, is good at stealth as well. He, too, like Solid Snake, is the sort of character who looks for affordances in the world where he can hide and sneak. But he is really no good at fighting in the open. He can do it, but not well enough for a player (or at least most of them) to win the game. So if a player has no effective ability for stealth games, he or she is out of luck. The player can either play another game or develop the effective ability (via learning from failure).

So players align with their avatars, rather than the game world directly, in order to take advantage of the avatar's effective abilities in the game world and the affordances that world offers that avatar. A player has to ask: What is Solid Snake good at? What am I good at that Solid Snake is also good at? How can I learn to take better advantage of Solid Snake's skills and tools (and the affordances they allow him to take up in the game world)? How can I be a better Snake? Can I discover things about Solid Snake or myself that make "us" better, or more innovative, or more interesting in the game?

Avatars in real life

Now I am going to say something that will sound odd. I have said that in games players align with the game world not directly but through their avatar. The avatar offers them a body, an identity, and a tool-kit in the game world.

Now I am going to claim that our human situation in the real world is similar. We humans do not align ourselves with the real world directly either. Rather, we align ourselves through an avatar, one that offers us a body, an identity, and a tool-kit that determines what affordances we must have the effective abilities to take up in the real world for accomplishing goals and solving problems.

Real life is like a video game. Video games are like real life. But in real life we tend to call our characters (the characters we are playing) "identities" or "roles" (Gee 2011, 2014a), not "avatars". We humans take on different identities in different contexts of our lives. One and the same person can talk and act, at different times and places, as an executive, a husband, a biker, a hip-hop fan, a gamer, and an African-American of a certain sort. Or one and the same person can talk and act, at different times and places, as a scientist, a wife, an avid distance runner, a radical feminist, and a 1.5 generation Korean American. We all have and must have multiple identities. We have to know how to talk and act in these identities. We have to "talk the talk" and "walk the walk" but differently in an executive boardroom than in a biker bar.

When humans talk and act in the world they talk in terms of an identity and they act out an identity. This is much like an avatar, though one they have usually had a hand in forming (we hope). And we humans each have many avatars. Thus, in real life we have to think about what we can do (about affordance-effective ability pairings) in terms of the "avatar" (identity or role) we are using. What executives can do and get away with—and how they can do things effectively—is different from what bikers can do and get away with and how they can do things effectively. They are as different as what Solid Snake can do is different from what Master Chief in *Halo* can do.

Our identities (avatars) mediate our consideration of affordances and effective abilities, just as Solid Snake's identity does for players. We align with the world not directly but in terms of some identity. People use different "moves" to threaten people when they are being an executive than when they are being a tough biker, even if they are one and the same person. They play different games with different avatars.

The identity of being an executive does not offer a good affordance for threatening physical violence, the identity of being a tough biker does. The identity of being a biker offers no affordance for manipulating stock prices, but the identity of some executives does. Note, too, that we have to earn the skills (level up) for our various identities (avatars) in the world as we do for many of our avatars in video games. Beginner bikers better know that they are just at the initial level of being a "real biker" and not take on hard challenges too quickly.

The fact that humans enact different identities in different ways lends life a certain game-like quality. We humans are used to existential questions like: Who is the real me? Is it all just a game? How much can I change or "mod" the identities I have or the roles I play in life? Can I "play" a given identity differently and better? Can I change it and transform it? Who is really controlling this "game"? Is it me, others, social institutions, or all of us? How much freedom do I really have?

Life is like a game, but, of course, it can be more consequential than any game. We play avatars in life (act out identities). The avatars we play—the identities we enact—can be looked at as bodies, identities, and took-kits just as they can for game avatars.

Imagine one and the same person is an executive, an African-American Texas barbecue master, and a devoted lover to his wife. Each of these identities requires the person to hold and dress and use his body differently. The person is physical and embodied in different ways in each identity and their characteristic contexts. Each of these identities is a different identity in the sense of way of being in the world with its own story and history. And each identity is associated with different skills, tools, and technologies that compose a distinctive tool-kit well fit to solve certain sorts of problems and not others.

So, since the identities by and through which we align to the world are really bodies, identities, and took-kits, perhaps we do need a new and broader name for them. We will call them (real world) "avatars". Life mimics games and games mimic life.

Conversations

We can now return to our ideas about conversations in the first chapter. There we saw that we can have conversations with others in language or with the world via actions (though, as we said, language is a form of action and people are worlds). We also saw that our conversations with the world involve a cycle of forming a goal, probing the world, reflecting on the world's response, and then acting again or rethinking our goal based on the world's response. We humans can, before and any time during this cycle, act things out in our heads and not in the world directly, via our mental ability to play video games in our heads.

We can now move on to discuss the role of affordances and effective abilities in our conversations with the world. When we form a goal and probe the world, we are looking for affordances of things in the world, affordances that we have the effective abilities (within the constraints of a given identity) to use to accomplish our goals. Sometimes, too, we are looking for the new things we need to learn in order to develop the right effective abilities. When we use our super power to simulate and role play in our minds to get ready for action and to avoid undue risks, we play out the search for affordance-effective ability pairings in our heads and use this "play" to later guide our probing of the real world.

What we have said about conversations with the world—about the probe-response-reflect-act again cycle and the video games we run in our minds to test actions—also applies to conversations we have with each other in language. Conversations in language are not all that different from conversations with the world. They are, in fact, quite similar, as we argued earlier.

In a conversation in language, we have goals we want to accomplish (e.g., bonding, informing, motivating, manipulating, or reassuring our listener or listeners). We probe our listener/s through moves in language (a form of action), reflect on their responses, and then act again based on these responses. We can and do simulate and role play in our minds before and during conversations to assess possible moves and lower the level of risk of failure (and loss of face). In conversations with others, the other is the "world" we are probing and we are in turn the other's world, since the other has goals as well when they respond to us and take their turn at talking.

We probe each other, though, in the guise of specific identities or enacting specific real world avatars. I carry out conversation with you differently when I am speaking as a professor to a graduate student than when I am speaking to you as a fellow birder (or gamer, or spouse, or Native American), even if we are the same people in both cases. Conversation in language is how we humans treat each other as social, cultural, and mental worlds to be explored.

In conversations with others we seek affordances in their attributes, abilities, desires, skills, character, and language resources for which we have the necessary effective abilities to use (yes, sometimes, manipulate) for our purposes (goals). For example, if you are very responsive to flattery and I have the ability to flatter well, this pairing can be effective in some cases for me to get the responses out of you I want or need. When we are romantically involved with someone, we see these matters quite clearly as we play video games in our minds and seek affordances for success in gaining love (and other things) as we talk and interact. In fact, this is part of what makes dating so exciting and nerve-racking at the same time.

So we are arguing that when we humans talk, when we act in the world, whether as part of everyday life or science, and when we play a video game, we are having interactive, responsive, turn-based, conversations based around the search for affordances we can use.

The question then becomes: Can we develop a unified theory of conversations in language, with the world, and in video games? That is, can we show that conversations in language, interactions with the world in everyday life and in scientific investigations, and video game playing are, at a deep level, similar (though not of course identical)? Better yet, can we learn more about them all by seeing their similarities worked out in different ways in different contexts?

So, let me summarize where we have arrived. We are going to use the framework below:

Affordance: **Effective ability:**

What something is good for   provided the user has the necessary ability

Affordance-effective ability pairings:

The search for affordances that a given type of user (e.g., a human being in a certain identity) has the effective abilities to use (or can learn).

Avatar:

A playable character in a video game or an identity a human takes on in a given situation or context. Avatars are bodies, identities, and took-kits used by players in games and us in the real world. Players and people in the real world align with the world (seek affordances they have the effective abilities to use) through their avatars, whether these be game avatars or real world avatars.

Conversation:

Interactive turn-taking responsive forms of communication between people in talk, players with a video game, or everyday people or scientists with the world. Such conversations are interactive, responsive to responses, and turn taking.

We need to be clear now that we are using the words "avatar" and "conversation" partly metaphorically and more widely than normal. We are doing this so that we can build a unified theory across the domains of talk, science, action in the world, and game playing. What we are really doing is expanding who we humans can have conversations with: we are adding to other humans as conversational partners the world and video games. We are also expanding the notion of human interaction to include acting not directly on other humans or the world as "I" alone, but in terms of a given avatar or social identity that creates possibilities and constraints about what we can and cannot do. In this sense, we are also expanding the notion of play, to talk about verbal conversations, conversations with the world, and video game playing as all forms of "games" we play with due deference for rules, conventions, goals, and often, too, a search for innovation.

What about games without avatars?

Our discussion so far has been centered on games with avatars and the ways in which our different identities in life function something like avatars do in games. But what about games without avatars, for example a game like *Tetris*? In *Tetris*, players manipulate falling blocks of different shapes and try to stack them at the bottom of the screen in a certain way. Players can turn the blocks as they fall and insert them into various positions in the stack at the bottom. The blocks have certain affordances; they can be moved and manipulated in certain ways and not others. Players must have—and almost all people do have—the effective abilities to use the controls to enact these moves and manipulations.

A game like *Tetris* is pure puzzle solving. In such a game, the player has no idea—and needs no idea—as to why he or she is solving the puzzles or what they mean beyond the pleasure of solving them. It is avatars and their accompanying stories that help players know specifically why they are doing what they are doing and what it means. So, Solid Snake in a *Metal Gear Solid* game, due to his identity and the story surrounding that identity, keys players into why they are engaging in stealth and seeking to solve certain problems. They are attempting to defeat bad guys who threaten to do nefarious deeds as part of a deep conspiracy. Snake is vastly outnumbered and, thus, must not go all "Rambo", but sneak and carefully plan his course of action.

In school, a subject like mathematics is often like a game without an avatar. It is pure puzzle solving where the students do not know why they are doing what they are doing and what it all means, beyond getting a grade, which is what substitutes for pleasure in much of schooling.

Students ought to know why someone would want to do math, what it means, and how good mathematicians (or engineers, architects, programmers, or anyone else who uses math for real) judge actions and problem solving in mathematics as an enterprise. To know this, students need to know what constitutes the identity (or one type of identity) of a mathematician or devoted math user of another sort. They need to know or learn why mathematicians or other sorts of devoted math users do mathematics, why they care about it, what they value in it, and how they judge what they consider a good or poor way to proceed when doing mathematics.

This identity is what we have called an "avatar". In a good math class it is an identity students take on, somewhat fictionally initially, in order to learn it and to play with it so they can eventually "own" it, transform it, and walk the walk and talk the talk of doing mathematics in some meaningful way. Just as with Solid Snake, identities connected to mathematics come with a story, in the case of mathematics these are stories about what different sorts of people and different types of knowledge do in the world and have accomplished.

Now puzzle solving and games without avatars can indeed be important and fun. And students can fruitfully play with mathematics as puzzles, if grades do not get too much in the way and they engage in math problems for the pleasure of it. Much of math is made up of beautiful puzzles just as *Tetris* is (indeed, go play the wonderful algebra game, *DragonBox*). Playing with math as a puzzle game is good for learning basic skills, for practicing skills, and for learning that math is as fun as *Tetris* if people have not scared you off with grading and talk of innate math abilities.

Nonetheless, it is hard to see how anyone could get to the higher levels of mathematics without understanding why certain sorts of people with certain sorts of goals have a great passion for mathematics or use it with great satisfaction. And to understand this is to understand the identities and values different people have who employ and enjoy mathematics. These identities each come with different preferred ways of doing things with mathematics that mediate how learners engage with mathematics as a contentful and meaningful enterprise in the world.

In the next chapter we will discuss avatars further. There we will argue that games like *Tetris* do, in a sense, have a minimal avatar. We will argue that all games, in reality, have avatars, though some have only a minimal one.

4

THE THINGS WE CAN BE

Avatars

In treating the identities people enact in their lives as "avatars", I am arguing that when you put on your suit to be a middle manager you are using a different avatar—one with different possibilities and constraints—than when you put on your biker gear and head off to a biker bar. In one case you "play" a middle manager (of a certain sort) and in the other case you "play" a biker (of a certain sort). Of course, this "play" can be serious and consequential.

This view of identity raises old and deep psychological and philosophical questions as to who the "you" is that is playing all these different avatars (identities). For example, consider the lines below from Hugh Howey's (2013) science fiction novel *Wool*. Holston, the sheriff in a futuristic society that lives in an underground silo, confronts his beloved wife as she seems to be going crazy and writhes on the floor yelling traitorous remarks that could lead to her death:

> "Lift her up," Holston said. His husband eyes swam behind tears while he allowed his dutiful sheriff-self to intervene. There was nothing for it but to lock her up, even as he wanted no more than room enough to scream.
>
> *(p. 24)*

Who is "he" that is both husband and sheriff? Who is the "he" that wants to just scream, husband, sheriff, or someone else?

As we said in the first chapter, we humans can imagine things in our heads. For example, we can imagine ourselves asking someone out on a date, perhaps as a way to get up the courage to actually do it. When we do this we are dividing ourselves into an "I" that imagines and an "I" that is being imagined as asking someone out on a date. You can even imagine your own funeral, a "game" in which you imagine yourself as a corpse.

Furthermore, for most of us humans, we have the sense that we can, while interacting with others, shine a little light down on our interaction and look down on ourselves from the outside, so to speak. We can look at ourselves interacting and make judgments about how things are going, how people are viewing us, and what we should or should not do. For example, as we try to convince the boss to give us a raise, we can, if we want, "see" the action from above like an onlooker and make adjustments. We can watch ourselves as we act in the world just as we can imagine ourselves acting in our head.

For each of us, barring mental health problems, there is an "I" that looks at ourselves interacting in the world (or simulates ourselves acting in our head), and another "I" who is acting in the world (or in our head). This division of self is the hallmark of human consciousness. Consider such sentiments as: I felt myself let go; I let myself go; I saw myself as if in a dream; I regretted who I had become; I lost control of myself.

The "I" who looks and the "I" who acts is a division in our minds that stems from the fact that we humans are consciously aware of ourselves as acting individuals. The "I" who looks—the "I" that can inspect what is going on as if from above like a little god—I will call our "conscious self". The "I" that the conscious "I" watches acting and thinks about in terms of whether things are going well or not, I will call the "acting I". The acting I is always acting out of, is always enacting one identity or social role or another, what I have called an "avatar".

One wrinkle with us human beings is that a great deal of what we think, feel, do, and choose stems from parts of our minds whose operations are not open to consciousness (Hood 2012; Macknit & Martinez-Conde 2010). The conscious "I" is privy to only a small part of what the brain has actually seen, felt, and decided. We never have awareness of all the facts of the matter and often do not even have awareness of the most important ones. Our conscious brain, our conscious I, often has to make up the best story it can about why "we" have acted, decided, or felt as we have in a situation. This story is rarely completely true, given that we are unaware of all the unconscious decisions and work other parts of our brain have done. In some cases, the story is largely false and leads to self-deception.

In some video games, the avatar is invisible. In the simplest case this happens when we a play a game in first-person perspective. In a First Person Shooter (FSP) we see, at best, our weapon and maybe our hand holding it. The illusion is that the player is standing in the space of the avatar, visible to others but partly invisible to ourselves as players, just as is true of our bodies in real life when we gaze out into the world.

Some games can be played in a third-person perspective. In this case, the player sees the body of his or her avatar as if the player was standing near the avatar and looking at the avatar. In some games, players can switch between first-person perspective and third-person perspective. The two modes make game play feel different and give game play a different sort of emotional valence.

In a video game the player is the conscious I and the avatar is the acting I. In this way, as in others, games externalize and duplicate how we think and act in the real world.

God games

However, there is another more interesting case where players do not see the bodies of their avatars. This is the case in games where players play god so to speak. In a game like *Civilization*, for instance, your avatar is not really presented on the screen. This is because in a game like this you are an all-seeing invisible "god". You have the tools to build, create, and destroy a civilization and everything in it. You move soldiers, ships, buildings, industries, vehicles, and other things, around the game world like toys. Indeed, such games have as one of their origins war games mapped out on table tops with toy soldiers and tanks.

In such games, players can manipulate the game to switch their perspective. They can see the game world "top-down" like a god looking down from the heavens or they can choose to see the action down on the ground from within the action as it goes on. The first view gives the player the big picture. The second view gives the player the look and feel of the action from the perspective of the actors (all the citizens and soldiers you have created and control).

In a game like *Civilization* or *Age of Empires* your avatar has no body or, rather, has an invisible displaced body like a god. But, nonetheless, your avatar has an identity (a world building, world destroying god-like figure or a general overseeing a whole war). And your avatar gives you a tool-kit to carry out a great many different types of actions, for example, to get miners to mine, soldiers to train and fight, to build armies and cities, to create religions, and to engage in diplomacy. All this is why games like this are often called "god games".

"God games" use this type of avatar because in such games players need to consider a whole world or system in "big picture" terms and make decisions about different parts of the world or system based on that big picture. In *Civilization* or *Age of Empires* the player is a world builder and destroyer. While players have no surrogate body in such games, they do often have a backstory that tells them what sort of god or leader they are (perhaps they are building Egyptian society across history) and why they are doing what they are doing.

In a game like *Tetris*, where you just manipulate falling blocks, we have the most minimal avatar. Players are just a mini-god with minimal abilities that they must use to their best effect. You are a puzzle-solving god, looking at a little self-enclosed world you can build and destroy. In a game like *Plants and Zombies* you are a somewhat more powerful god, manipulating all sorts of plants, each of which has a different affordance in the game, but nothing on the order of *Civilization* or *Rise of Nations*. In *Plants and Zombies* you have a tool-kit made up of different plants, each of which can protect your property in different ways from attacking zombies. Who is "ordering" the plants around? You are, the gamer as the "general" of an army of plants fighting zombie attacks.

Such games as *Tetris* and *Plants and Zombies* are mini-god games because the player plays a force or god that looks down on a world to make decisions in the context of the game world as a system that needs to be built up and sustained. In a game like *Tetris*—and indeed, in board games like *Monopoly*—you must be able to see and think of the whole and act in terms of it. This is characteristic of puzzle games in general.

When you play *Monopoly* who are you playing? You are playing some sort of capitalist, whether you yourself favor capitalism or not. There is something of a backstory in that we all know what it means to buy, sell, rent, and compete in a market place. In *Tetris* or *Bejeweled* we reach the limit of talk of invisible avatars. You have a top-down god like view of the field of play and you have powers to build, manipulate, and destroy. But you do not know why you are doing these things, save to solve puzzles.

We could, of course, just say such games have no avatars, visible or invisible. Or we can say the avatar is still a god like one, but now just a mini-god with a mini-world to control. Indeed, the deep enjoyment in such games is the feeling we humans get when we play such games that we have at least found a world, however small it might be, that we can control and play with. For many of us that is godly enough.

So sometimes the tool-kit we players use in a game is wrapped up in a visible avatar who is a character in the game. Sometimes the tool-kit is wrapped up in no visible character, but in a god like role in which we can build and destroy aspects of worlds. But even when we are gods we are constrained by the tools we have, tools which allow us to take advantage of the affordances of things in the game world provided we get adept at using the tools.

Do humans in the real world ever see themselves as acting in the world as a faceless, powerful, all-seeing god building and creating the world around them? Do world leaders and dictators ever feel they are playing a real-life version of *Civilization*? Can we look at ourselves not as "Joe" the executive, the biker, or the devoted husband, but as god or godly in the world, a maker and shaker and creator that is above and beyond mere mortals? Do we ever see ourselves as manipulating things from behind the scenes, a hidden, god-like, pervasive force that our "puppets" do not know personally?

Surely there are identities—like being a general or a president—that are "god like" in the way the avatar of god games is god like. And there are times where we humans all have to be leaders thinking of and acting on the basis of a big picture over which we have some control.

X-ray vision

Any actor in the world or avatar in a game has goals. To accomplish these goals actors or avatars (like Solid Snake) must develop and use what I will call "X-ray vision". Both the real world and some games come with quite beautifully detailed realistic graphics. But to solve problems in the world we humans have to see through or past these nice and copious details to pay attention to (to focus on) just the elements that are important for problem solving.

Solid Snake has to do the same in his world. He looks at the world in such a way as to see just the important details and patterns. In turn, Solid Snake trains and enables our way of looking at the game world as players. We must see the game world the way he does, through his eyes. We must see the important details and patterns that will allow us to act successfully. Snake has X-ray vision. He is attuned to the details that will afford him success. We players must learn Snake's way of looking at the world, his form of X-ray vision, a vision attuned to what in the world will help him and us accomplish his and our goals.

When you are playing *Metal Gear Solid*, what is important is where the guards are and where they are looking, what sorts of dark spaces and hiding spaces exist, and where there are open routes for escape. You (as Snake) have to strip the environment down to these basic elements in order to plan good strategies for successful action. This is X-ray vision. You are looking past irrelevant details to see where the affordances for successful action and problem solving are in the game world.

This is why games can be made with 2D graphics quite well or with 3D worlds that are not fully realized. Games can choose to do some of the work of X-ray vision for the player. Of course, the replete beauty of highly detailed game worlds can enhance enjoyment, aesthetic appreciation, and even a sense of realism and emotion, but when the player acts, he or she must act in a world stripped of irrelevant details and open to the expert X-ray vision of the avatar and the player.

Even when the player is being a god—as in *Civilization* or *Rise of Nations*—the player must see the essential aspects of the game world and interactions in it that will afford him or her (as a god or leader of a certain sort) success in the game. For example, the aspects of oceans that make them good for naval warfare are not the same aspects that make them good for rich fisheries. The place where you build a fort is not necessarily the place where you will drill for oil.

We humans, as we act on goals in the world, use X-ray vision, as well. We have to look through or past details to see the leverage points the world is offering us for accomplishing our goals. Like Solid Snake, sometimes we enhance this ability to seek and find the right details with new technological tools. A gardener must be able to look at a garden to see the signs of plant growth and health and the possibilities for new plantings. However, there is a device, based on night vision goggles, which allows gardeners to "see" the heat signatures of their plants, signatures which can help the gardener make judgments about which plants are healthy and doing well. Here the gardener sees what the unaided eye cannot see, while most of the other details in the world are vague and rendered mere background. This is a great example of X-ray vision.

Of course, as we humans act in the real world, we see what is important and what is not important in terms of the avatar we are playing (the identity we are enacting). Just like an avatar in a game, each identity (e.g., executive, gamer, biker, birder, scholar, etc.) we can enact comes with skills and tools to look at and act in the world in certain ways and not others.

Going mindfully meta

We said in the first chapter that scientists have conversations with the world. They probe the world based on a hypothesis and consider the world's response as a way to test their hypothesis. Based on the world's response, they revise their hypothesis or test it further until they have gotten ample evidence for it.

Scientists seek to understand how things work in their area of interest. How do cells work (biology)? How do stars work (astronomy)? How do societies work (sociology)? How do languages work (linguistics)? Since the world is a very complex place, scientists often build simulations or models of aspects of the world they are interested in, simulations and models which leave out unimportant or less important aspects of the world from the point of view of their particular interest. This, too, is a type of X-ray vision.

In fact, all thoughtful game play involves some degree of thinking like a scientist, at least informally and tacitly. Gamers test hypotheses and seek to figure how the rules in a game interact. But the phenomenon can morph into something different. Players can go what I will call "mindfully meta".

Going mindfully meta means: (a) thinking about something as a system; (b) seeking to understand in a conscious, overt way how the system works; (c) learning to articulate one's understanding in an appropriate and useful form of language; and (d) sharing knowledge with others so claims can be revised by others and knowledge can accumulate and spread. These processes involve thinking about what we do—especially about the taken-for-granted aspects of what we do—in an overt way. They involve, as well, building overt theories about a domain. I call this "going mindfully meta" because it crucially involves overtly thinking about—bringing to conscious awareness—things we often do only unconsciously, know tacitly, take for granted, or engage with on automatic pilot.

Humans in their everyday lives can choose to go mindfully meta about whatever they do in the world. They can stand back and seek to study the ways things work, how variables interact, how rules or conventions interact to create complexity. They can make models in their minds or on paper and seek to test them and revise them.

Of course, in some cases a meta stance towards games, interaction, or the world can spoil the pleasure of just being lost in play, acting, and interacting. Sometimes we can become too detached. But in other cases, life, interaction, and gaming can become too hard or too routine if we don't go mindfully meta.

So gamers often engage in their own "game studies" as they play, reflect on, and talk about games. "Going mindfully meta" towards games or interactions in and with the world is where "education" kicks in. As we advance, we seek out books or other kinds of information, we build our own rather abstract theories, and we develop and share specialist and technical forms of language with others who share our interests.

Going mindfully together: theory crafting

In the massive-multiplayer game *World of Warcraft* (*WoW*) (and others) some players engage, on Internet sites, in an activity called "theory crafting", sometimes written as "theorycrafting" (Paul 2011). *WoW* was for years the most popular massive-multiplayer game in the world, though it is somewhat in decline now.

Like all complex role-playing games, outcomes of any actions in *WoW* are the result of the interactions of many variables. Complex statistical models determine how these variables interact. The outcome of any action a player takes in battle, for instance, is an outcome of probabilities assigned to numerous interacting variables. Their interaction is complex enough, however, that emergent and unpredictable outcomes are possible. The system is so complex that even its professional designers do not fully understand its dynamics and they "tweak" (modify) the game continuously to achieve balance among the different classes and different styles of play.

Players who have a passion for studying the game often become expert enough to argue with the professional designers about how the system should be modified. They build tools for the game, called "mods", tools that millions of players use. These tools range from software that calculates a character's damage per second in a battle to devices that compile information to assist players in making decisions about what to buy and how to price items at the in-game auction house. Blizzard Entertainment, the company that makes the game, allows many of these fan-created "add-ons" to be downloaded and used in the game. Many such add-ons are now essential to game play for countless players.

Players who want to gain expertise in *WoW* often join with others, usually on the Internet, in an intensive sharing of knowledge about the game. They seek to understand its underlying statistical models. They study the best ways to design and play each type of character in different situations. They discover and share new game play strategies. They use highly technical knowledge to design new tools that improve game play and allow players to better understand what they are doing or should do. They are passionate about the game.

The study of a game like *WoW* as a system (seeking to understand how its underlying statistical models, variable interactions, and game mechanics work at the deepest level) is, as I have said, called "theory crafting" (see, for example, www. wowwiki.com/Theorycraft). Many players use the knowledge they gain from sites devoted to theory crafting to improve their play, and many contribute their own data and analyses to these sites that have become collaborative and communal repositories of knowledge.

Such sites also become "schools" to educate newcomers in theory crafting and to allow more expert players to hone their skills and knowledge further. There are, in addition, many other sites devoted to *WoW* that support other types of learning and knowledge building activities, but here I will concentrate on a site devoted to theory crafting called *Elitist Jerks*.

Elitist Jerks is a *WoW* discussion forum focused on the analysis of game mechanics and high-end raiding. The name "Elitist Jerks" is not intended ironically. The site has high standards for the format of discussions, and they are quite unapologetic about these standards. The introduction to the site states: "If you feel our rules are stupid or arbitrary, we don't really care. If you don't wish to follow them, you're welcome to return to the official Blizzard forums" (Boethius 2009).

One issue that concerns high-end *WoW* players is their "damage per second" (DPS). Some of the higher-end guilds in *WoW* demand that players achieve the highest possible DPS in raids. How much DPS a player achieves depends on many interacting variables, such as the player's (character's) race, class, equipment ("gear"), skills (of which each player has dozens), "buffs" (helpful spells cast on a player), and the speed and order with which the player uses spells.

Here is one post from *Elitist Jerks* meant to help players understand DPS at a deep and technical level. This post is long and highly technical, and we will look at only a small part of it. Here is what the post says just about melee damage, that is, fighting in close combat (Bikenstein & Malan 2008):

- Average weapon damage (**A**) can be calculated by adding the high and low ends of the damage range, then dividing by two.
- Weapon DPS is calculated by taking the average damage and dividing by the weapon speed (**S**).

$$DPS = \frac{A}{S}$$

- Crits – Melee crits are a chance to add 100% of the weapon damage. To add damage from critical hits the average damage is multiplied by the Crit percentage (**C**).

Below is what the post says about doing damage by casting spells. In this quote, "DoT" means "damage over time" (spells often do damage for a certain period of time after they are cast), HPS means "healing per second" (priests and some other classes can cast healing spells, spells that restore life points over time), and DD means "direct damage" (which usually refers to any type of magic spell whose direct effect is to cause burst damage—loss of life points—to one or multiple targets).

- Average spell damage is calculated the same way as weapon damage (high + low divided by two) for direct damage spells. DoT spells do not have damage ranges.
- Spell DPS (or HPS) is calculated by taking the damage divided by the cast time. DoT spells are calculated by taking the total damage divided by the total DoT duration. You may also want to include the cast time if there is no direct damage portion of the spell.
- DD + DoT spells will be DD/cast + DoT/duration.
- Spell crits – The chance to add 50% damage to a hit. To get the extra damage from spell crits, multiply the average damage by the Crit % and 0.5 (plus any talent/item Crit bonus modifier).
- Spell damage – This is a bonus to the damage of spells, for details on the co-efficient calculations, see the [Article]Spell Coefficients[/Article] article.

(ibid.)

There is no need for the reader to understand any of this. My point is that these excerpts are a formal analysis of a small aspect of DPS, itself only one small part of game play, based on a player's own research. I emphasize that this kind of analysis is now common. Entering "theory crafting" (or "theorycrafting") for *WoW* will bring up hundreds of thousands of hits on Google, many even more technical than the quotes above.

There are a number of points to make about theory crafting. First, a company (Blizzard) has created a complex system and its players study it using scientific and mathematical ways of thinking, as well as highly specialized uses of language. Yet it is not a complex system in the "real" world. Should we bemoan that these skills are being applied to a "play" system and not a "real world" one?

Second, these players are developing and using technical, technological, scientific, mathematical, research, analysis, collaboration, and argumentative skills that are the skills we hope people develop in school and that are central to work and life in the global, high-tech, complex-system-ridden twenty-first century. In this sense, the players' research is relevant to the real world.

Third, many people engaged in this research are amateurs. They need not, and many do not, have any official credentials in statistics, science, or computer science. Indeed, some are still in high school. On some sites such people engage with the professional game designers who designed and maintain *WoW*, arguing with them and contesting who has the best theory about how the game works or should work. In general, the amateurs are treated with respect by the professionals.

Fourth, this is very much a collaborative and community effort. Theory crafters discuss their work with each other and build on each other's work, sometimes disputing and contesting results, across the globe on fan-based Internet sites like *Elitist Jerks* and a great many others. Science itself is collaborative and communal, as well as competitive, so these players are engaged in a process resembling how actual scientists work.

Fifth, these theory crafters are not supported by any official institutions. They maintain their own standards internally. Participation is determined by interest, passion, and willingness to follow the rules. People of quite different ages and degrees of expertise can be present. People can contribute a lot or a little. They can largely consume or they can produce knowledge.

Sixth, there are many different sites devoted to theory crafting and other *WoW* related activities. Players have many choices. As *Elitist Jerks* says, if someone does not like their rules, there are other places they can go, including to official forums sponsored by Blizzard. Or they could start their own site.

Seventh, what these "amateurs" do affects how people play the game and, thus affects Blizzard, the company that makes the game. We will discuss below how player-made "mods" affect game play in significant ways. A company like Blizzard will change aspects of the game based on what players are saying and discovering about it. In a sense, the players are (free of charge) designing and re-designing the game and the way it is played. They are taking a certain type of "ownership" over the game.

Eighth, learning happens in a very interesting way on such sites. Learners can enter these spaces at any level of experience and be of different ages. They learn by joining a knowledge-producing community. They can learn in many different ways, for example through tutorials, discussion, their own research and problem solving, or didactic instruction offered by others. Their learning is in constant relation to game play, which motivates that learning and through which they can see in practice how what they have learned works. They are testing their hypotheses, theories, and what they have learned through tests or experiments in the game all the time.

When players take a mindfully meta and scientific stance to their gaming it, of course, does not always go this far. But the point is that gamers do not need certificates to theorize about their gaming. The same thing is happening in regard to many other activities in the real world. Everyday people, without credentials, are sharing information, doing research, and developing theories about a great many things such as health, diet and food, citizen science, gardening, birding, environmental issues, and many more.

Thoughtful humans have always theorized about their lives, interests, and circumstances. But today the Internet offers tools and many other people with whom anyone can take their theorizing further than ever before. They can compete with experts and becomes experts without any formal credentials.

When we develop, as we are here, a theory of discourse—that is conversations with people, games, and the world—we must be aware that "everyday people" without credentials have their own theories. They can compete with us professionals. We can learn a great deal from them, as well.

In a global, multicultural world, filled with new social media, "everyday people" (which we all are when we exit our professional identities) should go mindfully meta more often about human social interactions with others, with the real world, and with digital worlds. We should each develop our own ideas about discourse and our own ways of analyzing discourse. We should each theory craft our social worlds as a way to make our lives better, just as gamers theory craft to make their gaming better. We surely cannot leave these matters up to politicians, media talking heads, and academics more bent on developing careers than improving the world.

Summary: the things we can be

Below I summarize the "things we can be" or the "I's" we can inhabit in life, in language, and in games. I also list "X-ray vision", a concept we also discussed in this chapter:

The Conscious "I": The "I" that is consciously aware of what we do and seems to us to make choices and have free will. A good many of our human choices and feelings, however, are unconscious. Thus, the Conscious "I" is often having to "make up" ("fabulate") possible stories about why we are doing what we are doing or feeling what we are feeling. Our Conscious "I" can imagine things and design and play "video games" in our head. It can also watch ourselves as actors as if looking down from outside of an interaction or action.

The Unconscious "I": Not really a unitary thing, but the workings of a great many modules in the brain that process information, make decisions, and cause feelings without our knowing why or how. What gives the workings of all these modules some sense of unity to us humans are the stories we consciously tell about ourselves and our histories where we treat ourselves as responsible for our own actions and choices. These stories need not be true to ground us as actors in the world.

The Acting "I": The "I" that acts in our minds or in the world in the guise of one social identity or another or the "I" that acts in a game in the guise of an avatar.

Avatars: The identities we take up in life (such social identities as "biker", "honor student", "neo-liberal capitalist", and so forth) or the identities we take up in games (such as Solid Snake or the god running a civilization in *Civilization*).

Going Mindfully Meta: The conscious "I" acting and thinking as scientist trying to figure out how things work and why they work the way they do. Here we humans act as overt "theoreticians" and "model builders". We learn to pay conscious attention to aspects of the world we often take for granted and know about only tacitly. We can build and share knowledge collaboratively. This "I" requires no credentials. Much of our knowledge is tacit and unconscious. And, indeed, we need to honor such tacit knowledge and will never be able to learn how to articulate it all. Tacit knowledge is important to develop (through practice) and use. Nonetheless, people who rarely go mindfully meta, especially in our modern complex world, often exit the world too early on good Darwinian grounds. Going mindfully meta can be the basis of "critical thinking" and "critical literacy" if it is wedded to a proactive attempt to make our lives better and the world a better place based on a moral vision.

X-ray Vision: The ways in which we humans look through the rich details of the real world or a game world in order to see just what is important for our goals. How we look through the world to see just what is important for our goals is relative to the avatar we are "playing". That avatar gives us the perspectives, values, and tools from which and with which we act on and in the real world or the game world. Remember that we use the word "avatar" to cover both avatars in games (including god like ones) and social identities in the real world.

5

SYNTAX AND SEMANTICS

Syntax, semantics, and discourse analysis

The field of discourse analysis applied to video games does not yet exist. The question we are asking in this book is if it can exist. This question does not ask whether we can analyze games. Of course, we can analyze them in any number of ways as we can almost anything. However, to linguists discourse analysis builds on and goes beyond syntax and semantics (Gee 2014a, 2014b), two distinct levels of language. Discourse analysis takes as its beginning point "sentences" or "utterances" that have already been assigned a structure (syntax) in terms of basic grammatical units and a semantics in terms of the basic ("literal") meanings of these units.

Syntax is the set of rules or conventions by which a language's users combine words into phrases and phrases into clauses and sentences. How we combine things is part of what determines what things mean in language (an area covered by semantics). For example consider the examples below:

1 The destruction of my house in the fire took only an hour.
2 The fire took only an hour to destroy my house.

These two sentences say similar things, but in different ways. In (1) the subject of the sentence is "The destruction of my house in the fire", in (2) the subject of the sentence is "The fire". In (1) "the fire" is part of a prepositional phrase ("in the fire"). In (2) it is the subject of the sentence. In (1) "my house" is part of a prepositional phrase ("of my house"). In (2) it is the direct object of the verb "destroy". There are other differences in how words and phrases are made and combined in these two sentences.

Discourse analysis is the analysis of language in use. It has two jobs. Its first job is to ask (a) how things have been said and written, (b) how they could possibly have been said or written differently, and (c) what difference it makes that they were said or written the way they were rather than a different way.

So, for example, discourse analysts would want to know why someone would say (1) rather than (2) and what difference it could make in different contexts of actual use. Of course, to know how something was said or written and what alternatives there were to say or write it in a different way, we need to know the syntactical rules of the language (its grammar) and its semantics, that is, the basic meanings words and their combinations can have.

This first job of discourse analysis is really a question of design. We are asking why speakers or writers have used the grammar of their language to design their sentences the way they have and not some other way. How do the ways in which we design what we say allow us to accomplish goals, carry out actions, and communicate?

The second job of discourse analysis is to study how our sentences connect and relate to each other across time in speech or writing. As we speak or write we choose what words and phrases we will put into or "package into" sentences. The second job of discourse analysis is concerned with how various sentences, flowing one after the other in sequence, relate to each other to facilitate different interpretations in actual contexts of use.

For example, consider the three examples below:

3   The destruction of my home in the fire took only an hour.
4   My home was destroyed in the fire. It took only an hour.
5   There was a fire. It destroyed my home. It took only an hour.

Much the same information is expressed in (3), (4), and (5). However, that information is all combined into one sentence in (3), is expressed in two separate sentences in (4), and is expressed in three sentences in (5).

Why use (3) rather than (4) or (5)? This decision depends not just on what the speaker or writer wants to say, but on who the speaker or writer takes the listener or reader to be (e.g., friend, reporter, first responder, neighbor, stranger, etc.) and what he or she wants the listener or reader to feel, think, and possibly do (about the situation and about the speaker/writer). (By the way, some people claim there is no such thing as a "sentence" in speech, just in writing, where we see the sentences because they each end with a period. In my view, though, there are sentences in speech, though they are more flexible in speech than they are in writing.)

Syntax tells us the structure (or design properties) of sentences (that is, what are the sets of possible sentences in English). Semantics tells us what sentences and their constituent parts mean in a literal or basic sense. Discourse analysis (following from and going beyond syntax and semantics) studies how the design of sentences (their syntactic structures with their semantic interpretations) and how the sequence of sentences across time function in communication to invite certain sorts of contextually specific meanings responses in actual contexts of language in use.

More on the nature of syntax

Every human language is composed of many different styles of speaking and writing (Gee 2014a, 2014b). When they are being bankers, bankers use language in certain ways connected to the identities and functions of bankers. The same is true of bikers, birders, gamers, lawyers, engineers, teachers, and many more identities.

For example, in "everyday life" when speaking as an "everyday" (non-specialist) person, a person might say something like "Dogs sure vary a lot in how big they get". A specialist on dogs, say a biologist, might say something like "Canines display a significant amount of variation in how large they grow". These are two different styles of language, two different ways with words, used by different people for different purposes.

I will call any distinctive style of a language a "social language" (the term "register" is also sometimes used here). Consider the text below from a *Yu-Gi-Oh* card:

Cyber Raider
Card-Type: Effect Monster
Attribute: Dark | Level: 4
Type: Machine
ATK: 1400 | DEF: 1000

Description: When this card is Normal Summoned, Flip Summoned, or Special Summoned successfully, select and activate 1 of the following effects: Select 1 equipped Equip Spell Card and destroy it. Select 1 equipped Equip Spell Card and equip it to this card.

This is clearly in a special variety of language—what we might call "*Yu-Gi-Oh* language". This is a social language. It is technical or specialist in the same way the language of academics or lawyers is. *Yu-Gi-Oh* language—like all social languages—exists to allow *Yu-Gi-Oh* players (people enacting the identity of being a *Yu-Gi-Oh* player or even a *Yu-Gi-Oh* fanatic) to do the things they need to do to play *Yu-Gi-Oh*. Social language exists to allow certain sorts of people (e.g., doctors, physicists, game members, etc.) to do the special things they do when they are engaged in their interest or job.

So when we ask why a sentence or set of sentences is designed the way it was and not some other way, we are asking a question about style and design. Syntax is about units (words) and combinations of units (phrases and sentences). Semantics is about the basic meanings of these units and combinations of units. Discourse analysis asks how these units and their combinations and their sequence and flow across time, in actual contexts of communication, signal a particular social language and carry out actions or tasks (work) associated with that social language.

So if video games are open to discourse analysis we have to be able to identify their units and how they combine, what they basically mean, and what sorts of styles ("social language") these units, their combinations, and their sequence or flow through time create to carry out distinctive actions and tasks. This is an issue to which we now turn.

The world and games

Does the world have a syntax (a grammar)? Do video games have a syntax (a grammar)? These questions amount to asking whether we can study the world or video games as if they were designed, as if they had parts that combine by regular "rules" into patterns. It is, of course, clear that video games are designed. And I will later argue that games are composed by combinations of units (like words and phrases) that make up patterns that are meaningful to players. And surely games have different stylistic variations to set up different types of play.

But is the world designed? If you think God designed it, then it is designed for you. But even if you think the world evolved, scientists have discovered that they can study the world as if it was designed. They can see parts and combinations of parts that seem to combine by "rules" into larger patterns that have meaning or significance (in different ways) to humans, animals, and to scientists in terms of how to act, understand, and survive in the world. This is why we can have conversations with the world and why it is very important to respect what the world "says" back to us when we act in the world or probe it.

Now the world is not "well designed" in the sense that a designer could not have engineered many things in the world more efficiently (Gould 1980). Evolution has to build from what has come before. It cannot remake the Panda's thumb when environmental change means Pandas need to hold and eat bamboo to survive. Nonetheless, evolution is still a building process that has to follow the rules of physics and biology and—perhaps quite surprisingly—often the rules of mathematics.

So, let's start with this question: Can there be a discourse analysis of video games? As I said earlier, there is no doubt that we can analyze the meanings and import of games, as we can any cultural artifact. My question is more specific. Discourse analysis is a part of linguistics. It is intimately tied to the way language works as a structural and communicational system. So my question is related to the question as to whether video games bear enough similarity to language to be open in some insightful way to discourse analysis. This question amounts to a yet bigger one: How far can communication stretch beyond language and, thus, how much are other sign systems (e.g., mathematics, programming languages, and video games) like language and vice-versa?

To start, consider the images (screenshots) from *Metal Gear Solid* games below:

Thanks to the way the human eye works, any visual scene is composed of shapes, angles, and lines that we humans then compose (in our brains) into recognizable objects (Marr 1982, 2010). The image that hits our eyes is two-dimensional (and upside down) with no clearly demarcated edges and boundaries. Our eyes and brains work together to turn these images into identifiable shapes, with clear edges and boundaries and identities.

Figure 5.3 shows a realistic looking screenshot from *Metal Gear Solid*. Figure 5.2 shows a less realistic looking scene. Figure 5.2 contains 3D blocks instead of any more realistic and detailed depiction of what the blocks are. It does, however, depict a guard and Solid Snake realistically. This image is used for training. Players can learn to operate Solid Snake (their avatar) in terms of hiding and escaping by being

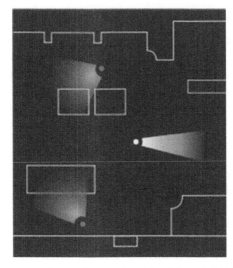

FIGURE 5.1 Representation of the soliton radar, *Metal Gear Solid* (Game Boy)

FIGURE 5.2 Metal Gear Solid VR Missions ISO (An expansion pack for the original *Metal Gear Solid*)

taught how to see the world in terms of the spatial details that are important for action in this sort of game (hiding and escaping).

Figure 5.1 shows a yet further reduction of a scene. Figure 5.1 is a two-dimensional drawing with, in the game, red dots (indicating enemies), a white dot (indicating Solid Snake) and colored cones of light (indicating range of vision for the enemies and for Solid Snake). Figure 5.1 is actually used in the game. It is an image from a radar device Solid Snake wears. It is seen in Figure 5.3 in the top right corner and is used by the player (as Solid Snake) as a map to plan strategy and orient spatially in the game.

I will call an image like Figure 5.3 a "realistic image". However, keep in mind that realistic images in games and in the world are the products of work by our eyes and brain, not given to us directly.

FIGURE 5.3 Metal Gear Solid: The Twin Snakes

An image like Figure 5.2 I will call a partial "3D Sketch". This image could go further by depicting the guard and Solid Snake as 3D blocks of some sort, in which case it would be a total 3D Sketch. 3D Sketches leave out a lot of detail to focus on aspects of the game world important for action and accomplishing goals.

I will call an image like Figure 5.1 a "2D Sketch". Since the world we live in is 3D, 2D Sketches always leave out many aspects of the real world or any realistic depiction of it.

Thanks to the way the human brain processes images, any realistic image can be decomposed into a 3D Sketch and any 3D Sketch can be decomposed into a 2D Sketch. This is so because when we see the world or any realistic depiction of it, the eye first sees a vague bounded 2D image (that is what is on the retina) and has to mentally compose it into a more sharply bounded set of 2D shapes and then into a 3D image composed of clearly bounded spaces and objects. We then have to identify these spaces and objects in terms of what they are, not just as shapes, but in terms of cultural categories like humans, animals, robots, and corridors. So moving from a realistic image (like Figure 5.3) to a partial 3D Sketch (like Figure 5.2) to a 2D Sketch (like Figure 5.1) just reverses the process.

But why would we ever want to go "backwards" and decompose a realistic image into a simpler image? Why would we want to use an image like Figure 5.1 or Figure 5.2 rather than the realistic image in Figure 5.3? We saw in the last chapter, when we want to accomplish goals in a video game (or the real world), we have to use "X-ray vision" to see through the rich details of 3D images to focus on just the details that are relevant for accomplishing our goals. The relevant details are sometimes lines, edges, angles, and other spatial patterns (and not the full wealth of detail in the world or in an image) that help direct action in the right ways.

Sometimes, seeing Figure 5.3 as more like Figure 5.1 (turning 5.3 into 5.1 in your mind) is important to successful action in a game. In a game like *Metal Gear*

Solid there are times when it is effective just to pay attention to lines of sight, patterns of light and shadow, and bounded corridors of space. As we prepare for action we care where the guards are looking, not how tall they are. We care about routes of escape, not about the decorations on the walls. We care about whether Snake is well hidden, not what his costume looks like (no matter how cool it is).

Because 2D images or 3D Sketches can be more useful for directing our attention and allowing us to engage in successful actions, games can perfectly well be made with 2D graphics or 3D Sketches, even graphics made of very simple lines and moving shapes. A game could be made solely out of images like Figure 5.1. In that case, our avatar (Solid Snake) would just be a white point of light. Indeed, we will eventually have to ask why fully realistic graphics are so often used in games and what they do for us as players. After all, to play we often have to ignore a good many of their details and focus on just those details important for our actions and problem solving.

Paying attention to the beautiful ponds in *Far Cry*, with their colorful fish, will just get you killed. You must quickly scan the environment for enemies, places to hide, and the best ways to attack your foes. So why have the ponds and the pretty fish? We will take up this question later.

The syntax and semantics of games

The world has a syntax and semantics for us humans thanks to how human vision works. The eye sees the world in vaguely bounded 2D (upside down) images. The eye and brain then process this image to construct 3D images with bounded edges and clear shapes. These edges, angles, and bounded surfaces and the way they are combined into spaces and objects (and actions across the flow of time) constitute the syntax of the world for us humans. We then assign names and conceptual labels to the spaces and objects and actions, based on cultural knowledge and social conventions. This is the semantics of the world for us humans.

Scientists have special tools that allow them to see the world in a different way than do "everyday people". With their telescopes and microscopes, they see different units (like atoms, cells, and stars) that combine in different ways (into molecules, organs, and galaxies). The world for them has a different syntax and semantics.

Games are made out of a flow of visual images. So they share the syntax and semantics of the human visual world. But like scientists gamers have special tools that allow them to see the game world in a different way. Gamers have controllers and avatars through which they can manipulate the game world to accomplish goals and solve problems. Thus, they see the game world not just in terms of spaces, objects, and actions, but in terms of what these things in the game world are good for in terms of accomplishing their goals for winning the game and solving its problems.

Gamers see the game world in terms of what we can call "game mechanics". Game mechanics are what you can do with things in a game. So gamers see the game world in terms of verbs (actions): crates are good for breaking, ledges are good for jumping, shadows are good for hiding, and so forth. Additionally, things in game worlds can combine in various ways to enable certain actions. For example, a ledge, gap, rope, and wall can in some games combine to enable a deft set of moves to get across the game world (as in *Tomb Raider* games, for example).

The syntax of games is composed of the objects and spaces relevant to action. The semantics is a conceptual labeling of these spaces and things not just in terms of their real world identity (e.g., a crate) but in terms of what they are functionally good for in the game (e.g., breakable to get a power up).

Thus, gamers bring special tools to the visual world of the game, not microscopes and telescopes, but things like avatars (remember they see the visual world through the avatar's skills) and controllers that allow them to manipulate the game world in various ways. Just as a physicist can "see" atoms and molecules, so, too, gamers can see "places where I can jump to", "walls I can climb", "objects I can break", "locks I can pick", "enemies I can stealth kill", "shadows I can hide in", and so on and so forth,

When gamers combine units into larger patterns (like words into phrases and sentences) and assign them meanings in terms of game actions, they create things like "red wooden rectangle (= a box) is breakable", "jumpable gap", and "corridor for escape". Gamers see game worlds in terms of how the images and possible actions in the game world can be used to solve problems.

Games speak to players in terms of affordances for action. Players speak back to games in actions. They carry on a conversation with the game about how to accomplish successful actions and accomplish goals. The syntax of games are the "rules" for combining objects with affordances for action. The semantics of games are the actions these objects and their combinations can afford for us players in terms of our effective abilities (thanks to our avatar).

Semantics (meaning)

We will now go a bit more deeply into semantics. Semantics in language deals with the "literal meanings" of words and the phrases into which they combine or, better put, with the range of possible meanings a word or phrase can have in actual contexts of use as these are constrained by the basic or core meaning of the words or phrases (Gee 2014a).

For example, a sentence like "The cat died" means at the semantic level something like: A FELINE THING BECAME NOT ALIVE. "Literal meanings" are the sorts of meanings listed in dictionaries (or "the lexicon" in linguists' terminology). So, too, in games, a game's semantics is what the objects on the screen depict in a literal sense (e.g., breakable crate). Meaning in language and in games involves much more than just semantics, as we will see below. There are other sorts of meaning. In an actual utterance in a specific context—like "Look at the cat float across the sky"—"cat" could mean a cloud shaped like a cat.

How is semantics (basic interpretation) accomplished in language? We speakers carry around in our heads what logicians call "universes of discourse" (Goldfarb 2003).

A universe of discourse is a theory of what exists in a particular world or reality. It is the set of objects and their properties that we take to exist in a given domain.

So, for example, for the culture I am a part of, in the domain of the world of mythology there are things like unicorns, fairies, goddesses, and many other such things, each with various properties or attributes. This is my universe of discourse for mythology. In the universe of discourse for the "real world" (meaning what physically exists)—again, for my culture—these things do not exist. In my real world universe of discourse, there are things like rocks, birds, and chairs, each with their own properties.

A sentence like "Unicorns have one horn" is interpreted semantically in terms of my mythology universe of discourse. The word "unicorn" refers to unicorns and "horn" to the sort of horn I have seen in pictures of unicorns. A sentence like "Narwhals have one horn" is interpreted semantically in terms of my real world universe of discourse. The "narwhal" refers to a species of whale people have discovered and studied and "horn" to the sort of horn they actually have (which, then, too, I myself have actually only seen in pictures).

We humans have in our heads many different (culturally variable) universes of discourse, each a "theory" about what exists in a given domain or realm. I have, for example, a universe of discourse for mythology, for the real world, for baseball (none for cricket), for romance, and for science fiction, and others. (In some people's universe of discourse for romance, a sentence like "John is Fred's husband" has no literal meaning, since in their universe of discourse for romance, males with husbands do not exist, so the word "husband" here can be assigned no meaning for these people. Other people have a universe of discourse for romance that makes "John is Fred's husband" perfectly meaningful.)

Where do people get the various universes of discourse in their heads? They get them from the stories their cultures or smaller social groups tell and theories these cultures or groups hold. For example, expert birders have terms for specific types of feathers on birds that I cannot even see. I have no universe of discourse for these feathers. Even if I knew their names, I could not assign them a name, because for me they do not exist in the right way, that is, in any way I could identify them in reality. Of course, I could learn and I would do so by learning from the stories, theories, and practices of such expert birders. We pick up new universes of discourse from talking to and interacting with people who have them.

So now we have discussed how words and phrases in language are assigned meanings (semantic meanings, basic meanings). Of course, our universes of discourse for language allow us to assign some meanings to things in games. I do not need to be a gamer to know that the image of Solid Snake is a human and probably a man. However, we cannot know who he is—cannot interpret him as Solid Snake—unless we know what I will call the game's universe of discourse. So, games, too, get their basic meanings from universes of discourse, just like language does.

What I mean by a game's "universe of discourse" is all the characters, places, events, and objects associated with a game (or series of games). It is, just as it is for language, the set of things and their properties and relationships that exist in the game world. Thus, the *Metal Gear Solid* universe is made up of the Metal Gear characters, places, events, and objects in that story.

What determines a game's universe of discourse? What determines it is the story in the game (or set of related games). The story keys us into what exists in the game world, what properties each thing has, and how they relate to each other. The story teaches us the universe of discourse for the game world.

An important and special part of a game's story is its avatar. The avatar determines what can be done (in terms of skills) and, thus, too what things in the world are good for in terms of action. If the avatar cannot jump then nothing in the world is jumpable. The avatar is also, as we saw earlier, a tool-kit of things that can be used for problem solving, including the avatar's skills, but also things like radars, maps, and tools (like lock picks, keys, and night vision goggles).

Take as an example the image in Figure 5.1. This sort of image is part of the *Metal Gear Solid* universe of discourse. It is the sort of image that Solid Snake's radar device creates. The game's story tells us that the radar exists and how it operates. Thus, we players can map the red dots into "enemies" or "guards", the white dot into "Solid Snake", and the colored cones into cones of sightlines. This process would assign the sentence-like meanings "Guard looks at container" and/or "Guard can see container", and "Guard cannot see Solid Snake", and others, to the image, even though the image is not at all realistic.

A game's universe of discourse, as this is determined by its story, is not, though, just a set of things that exist in the game world. The game's story exists in large part to tell us not just what exists, but what properties for action the things that exist have. Solid Snake is not just Solid Snake, hero and man, but a fictional person/avatar with certain skills and tools, useable for accomplishing goals in the game in certain ways. The story keys us into what Snake can do and why he—and, thus, us players—wants or needs to do it. A game's universe of discourse is a set of things, characters, and an avatar as "affordances for and explanations for action". A given game world may not just have crates in it, it may also have "power ups" that can be inside crates that, therefore, need to be broken. It importantly has breakable and non-breakable crates.

Games without stories

So what about games without stories? What about a game like *Tetris*? *Tetris* has a "syntax" (a grammar). We can clearly see the units ("words")—they are various sorts of shapes—and how they can be combined together. But *Tetris* has no semantics. We have no idea—and do not care—what the shapes stand for or mean. Without a story, there can be no universe of discourse and, thus, too, no semantics.

Of course, in *Tetris* we do interpret the shapes as squares and various types of rectangles. But this is an interpretation based on our universe of discourse for geometry or everyday perception of the world. This is a semantics, but it is not distinctive to a game world.

It is, of course, possible to say that *Tetris* does have a story, but just a very minimal one. The story could be said to be "Blocks are falling and need to be stacked in just the right way or they disappear and eventually something bad happens, namely the game ends and you lose." This does, admittedly, give a minimal meaning (semantics) to *Tetris*. It does determine a minimal universe of discourse unique to *Tetris* (e.g., things like "hard block to stack", "block that must be turned just so", "risky stack on the bottom", and so forth exist). So, just as we saw earlier that we could say a game like *Tetris* has a minimal avatar (instead of none)—a sort of mini-god—we can say, too, it has a minimal story (and, thus, too semantics).

So I am happy to say that games without stories have no semantics or a minimal one. In any case, it is clear that part of the pleasure of a game like *Tetris* is near pure play with syntax—with forms or structures combining in certain ways—and not any very interesting story. This is also a source of pleasure for some sorts of mathematicians, grammarians, and artists in their work.

Summary

In the next chapter, we will see that discourse analysis really gets going only after syntax and semantics are done and is built on them as a foundation. We have argued here that language, the world, and games each have a syntax or grammar. This means that we can identify units (or basic parts) and the ways they combine to make bigger units or patterns. Scientists have tools that allow them to see units (e.g., atoms) and larger combinations (e.g., molecules) and rules of combination that we "everyday" people do not see. Gamers do too.

For us everyday people, the basic units in the world are the basic lines, angles, edges, and shapes that we construct from the patterns of light and dark that hit our retina. We combine these elements into objects and assign them culturally based meanings. The grammar of vision (the work of eye and brain) determines how this is done. Of course we use this grammar to see and interact with images in the world and in media, including games.

The syntax or grammar of games as game designers design them and players play them is composed of patterns of shapes and objects and action that have implications for the goals players need to accomplish. We will deal with this more in the next chapter. Such patterns are identified by players using their X-ray vision to see through copious details to just the aspects of the game world that are important for action and accomplishing goals. The syntax and semantics of games are all about how things can combine to make actions happen. They are all about game mechanics.

The ways units combine in language and in games create distinctive styles ("social languages") that fit with the "work" (purposes, tasks, actions) people and gamers need to get done. Style is not just aesthetic, it exists as well to let lawyers write briefs and contracts, some game designers to make platformers and others to make real-time strategy games.

The anthropologist Claude Lévi-Strauss (1968) once said that mythology treats objects in the world as "good to think with". By this he meant that myth can treat things like cooked food as a sign or symbol of culture versus raw food as a sign or symbol of nature. It can treat ravens as messengers from the dead, thunder as messages from the gods, and mountain tops as places to commune with the ancestors. In this way objects can be weaved into stories about creation, ancestors, origins, and spiritual matters.

So, too, gamers treat objects as "good to act with". They weave stories—and here I mean the player's story of his or her own choices, actions, failures, and accomplishments—out of objects seen as combinable and useful for actions, actions that can make a player a hero or, at least, a distinctive actor in a distinctive world, for example, one sort of Solid Snake.

6

SITUATED MEANING

Situated meaning

In language, a syntactic structure like $_S$[Noun Phrase $_{VP}$[(Verb) Noun Phrase)]$_{VP}$]$_S$ can be filled in with words to make the sentence: "A man slapped the guard". The semantics of this sentence is derived from the literal meanings of "a", "man", "slap", "the", and "guard". The syntax (the rules by which words are combined into phrases and phrases into sentences) directs the semantics, as well, to derive the meaning "AGENT = a man + HIT WITH OPEN HAND = slapped + AFFECTED OBJECT = the guard". This all follows from "rules of grammar", which are the conventions by which syntax and semantics work.

However, any sentence when used as an actual utterance takes on much more meaning beyond the level of literal meaning (semantics). We give further and deeper interpretations to words and utterances in actual contexts of use. We add layer after layer of meaning to them based on how we construe the context in which we are communicating. We also interpret words and utterances more deeply in terms of the utterances that precede and follow them in actual speech (a special kind of context, namely linguistic context).

Discourse analysis analyzes language in use and deals with meanings that go beyond semantics and involve context and inference (Gee 2014a, 2014b). It studies three closely related things. Repeating in a different way what we have said before, we can call these "packaging", "flow", and style ("social languages").

First, discourse analysis studies how things are said and written and how they could have been said or written differently and what difference it makes that they were said or written the way they were. For example, why does someone say or write "It took only an hour for my house to burn down in the fire" versus "My house took only an hour to burn down in the fire". In these two sentences information is packaged (combined) in different ways, using the syntactic resources of language.

Second, discourse analysis studies how sentences connect, combine, and pattern across the sequence and flow of time in written or spoken language in use. For example, why does someone say or write "My house took only an hour to burn down in the fire" (one sentence) versus "My house burned down in the fire. It took only an hour" (two sentences) versus "There was a fire. My house burned down. It took only an hour" (three sentences).

Third, style is a matter of how the resources of language—its units and combinations of units—can pattern into different varieties useful for certain distinctive purposes, tasks, or actions. So carpenters, *Yu-Gi-Oh* players, lawyers, linguists, gang members, and anime otaku develop their own special ways with words and phrases, their own distinctive styles of language, ones fit for the work or interests they engage in. Of course, these styles all use some resources from the vernacular version of the language, but they also add special words, phrasings, and grammatical patterns to mark out their identity and to engage in their distinctive work or play. In other work (Gee 2014a, 2014b), I have called these distinctive language styles "social languages" (varieties of language used by distinctive social groups for their distinctive purposes).

Discourse analysis studies packaging, flow, and style in order to explicate "situated meaning" (sometimes called "utterance token meaning"). Situated meanings are the meanings words, phrases, sentences, and sequences of sentences take on in actual contexts of use. Semantics deals with literal meaning, or, better put, the meaning ranges (possibilities) of words, phrases, and sentences (this is sometimes called "utterance type meaning"). For example, at the semantic level, the word "coffee" means anything to do with the substance coffee. In actual contexts of use the word can have different situated meanings. For example: "The coffee spilled. Go get a mop (liquid)"; "The coffee spilled. Go get a broom (grains or beans)"; "The coffee spilled. Stack it again (tins)"; "I'll have coffee ice-cream (a flavor)"; "Big Coffee is as bad as Big Oil (an industry)".

Situated meanings are determined by what speakers/writers and listeners/readers take as relevant aspects of context. Situated meanings are also determined by shared cultural knowledge. Such cultural knowledge has been studied under terms like "folk theories", "cultural models", "figured worlds", "schemes", "frames", and others (Duranti 1997; Gee 2014a; Holland et al. 1998). Thus, discourse is also related to the study of cultures and other social groups that share knowledge and practices with each other.

Games and discourse analysis

Thus, the question "Can there be a discourse analysis of video games?", taken literally, asks whether games have a syntax (a grammar), semantics, packaging, flow, style, and situated meanings based on contexts of play and associated social and cultural knowledge. If they do, they are in that sense "like language" and open to discourse analysis.

Take as an example Figure 5.3 from Chapter 5 (see p. 41). In the context of actually playing the game and my knowledge about this and other *Metal Gear Solid* games (they are primarily, but not entirely, stealth games) and in terms of the ongoing sequence or flow of the images in the game, I construe this image to mean not just "Solid Snake looks down a corridor" (its "semantic" or "literal meaning"). I construe it to mean as well something like: "Solid Snake is wary of what might be around the corner of the corridor; it could, perhaps, be a guard, a machine gun turret, or an alarm. He is preparing a plan to engage in stealth to attack without being seen or to evade trouble altogether" (and, indeed, much more even than that).

Furthermore, since this is a game and I am a gamer (both of these are just more parts of the context), I also construe this to mean "I myself as Solid Snake am wary of what might be around the corner of the corridor and I should be preparing a plan (based on the game mechanics available to me, which are just the actions available to Snake) to engage in stealth and I better consult the radar image". This mixture of me as gamer, Snake, game mechanics, and actions both I and Solid Snake can take in the virtual world is the heart of gaming.

Now we pointed out in an earlier chapter that games can perfectly well be made from simple 2D images. So, why bother with the expense of making more realistic images as in Figure 5.3? One reason is that such realistic images facilitate the work of construing situated meanings. They enrich the context. But they are not necessary.

The grammar and discourse of games can operate perfectly well on 2D Sketches or 3D Sketches. This gives us, perhaps, "minimal games", but often good games nonetheless. Such "minimal games" also offer us an excellent place to start in developing a theory of discourse analysis for games. We can see the essentials and tell the forest from the trees, though we will have to return eventually to games made from realistic images.

Thomas Was Alone

I will turn now to a discussion of discourse in games by using the game *Thomas Was Alone* (*TWA*). *TWA* is a game that uses simple 2D images as its screen images. *TWA* is a pretty minimal game, but, nonetheless, it still has a semantics. Consider the screenshots (Figures 6.1 and 6.2) from *TWA*.

These screen images are composed of lines, solid black blocks, and small colored rectangles. The closest we get to a realistic image is the "water", the white block with a wavy top in Figure 6.1.

If you play *TWA*, or even look at the images above, you can see that the small colored triangles are like words (they can be separate and act separately) that can be combined together (like a phrase) as in Figure 6.1, where red is on top of orange and orange is on top of yellow and yellow is on top of blue. So red-orange-yellow-blue (going top down) is an acceptable combination ("sentence").

Order matters in a minimal way. Each shape can be moved independently and each has different skills, e.g., being able to jump very high (yellow), being able to move across water (blue), being able to jump down rather than up (green), and so forth. However, when they are combined, the bottom one determines the movement (it is the only one the player can move, and the others move along

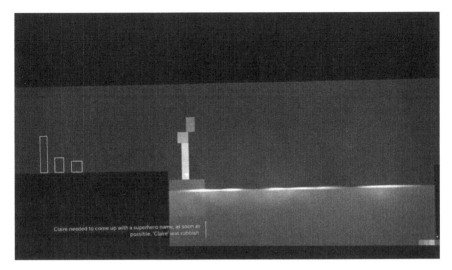

FIGURE 6.1 Screenshot from *Thomas Was Alone*

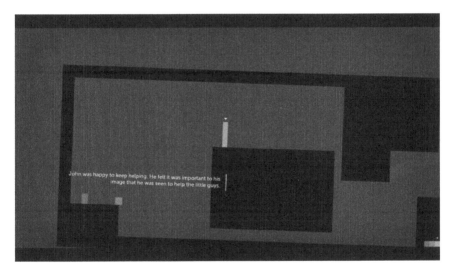

FIGURE 6.2 Screenshot from *Thomas Was Alone*

with it, on top of it). In a sense, the bottom shape acts like a predicate (verb) in language.

The open white rectangles on the top left of Figure 6.1 are the goal states. When each is filled with the appropriate shaped rectangle, the level ends and a new one begins. Black surfaces are ones any shape can move along and the "water" shape is an area that only the large blue square can move along without "dying".

Notice that all I have done so far is interpret the images in terms of the game's game mechanics, which is, indeed, part of its semantics, part of the process of interpreting the elements or parts of images in the game in a basic literal sense. This is enough semantics to make the game a game, though a fairly minimal one. But without using more visual details or the game's story-based universe ("ontology") we cannot go any further with semantic interpretation. If there was no more semantics to *TWA*, it would be a game like *Tetris*.

However, *TWA* does have a game universe that determines its ontology, though its universe is minimal. *TWA* has a narrator whose narration is heard and whose words are printed on the game screens (though not all screens are narrated or have print on them). This narrated story is pretty much all that determines an ontology for *TWA*.

Within the story each shape has a name and something of a backstory as an artificially intelligent agent inside a mainframe computer whose programming has gone awry. The shapes are trying to escape and get out of the computer. In an interesting twist, each shape has certain unique abilities and limitations (determined by the game's game mechanics) that fit with the character's personality traits and role in the story.

For example, Thomas, the red rectangle, has an up-beat attitude and can do an average jump. John, the yellow rectangle, is arrogant and eager to show off and can jump quite high. Claire, the blue square, who starts off feeling badly about herself but comes to see herself as a superhero, cannot jump well or move fast, but she can float and move in water and thereby save others by giving rides across water. Chris, the small orange square, has a dismal attitude and has a low jump height and a slow movement speed. There are other characters as well. Here we see a mapping among (a match among) shape (the elements of the 2D Sketches that make up the game), game mechanics, and role (function) in game and story.

In *TWA*, the narration (as well as some un-voiced quotes from programmers and others involved with the company behind the computer system Thomas and his friends are inside of) offers a universe that determines the game's ontology and allows us to assign literal meanings and basic functions to each shape and the backgrounds along which they move and jump. In this way, the game's semantics is determined. We now assign the red shape the meaning "Thomas, the average jumper". We assign the blue shape the meaning "Claire (who feels bad about herself), the shape that can cross water".

Situating meaning in *TWA*

Let us now move on to see how contextually sensitive meanings and inferences— situated meanings—work in *TWA*. Situated meaning allows us to go well beyond basic semantics in giving meanings to the game and our game play.

TWA's game universe is determined by its narration. However, the narration is also printed on the screen. This means that the oral words of the narration are not really doing much as oral words *per se*, since they are visually apparent (and longer lasting and quicker to read than they are to listen to) on the screen. So what is the oral narration offering? Why even have it at all? Why "waste" money paying a voice actor?

Oral language is composed of words and phrases and sentences. These can all be written. But oral language also has "intonation". Intonation is the tone, pitch, and variation of the voice as it speaks (is "voiced"). These are not written; they are left out of written language. Intonation is the "musical" part of language and it works differently (has different functions and meaning) in different languages. In English, intonation carries information about dialect, attitude, emotion, and what parts of an utterance are foregrounded (as the focus of attention) and what parts are backgrounded (as background information), as well as other functions.

Since *TWA* prints the words of the narration on the screen, this, in a way, subtracts the words from the oral narration and means that they really only function there (in the oral narration) to carry the intonation of the narrator's voice, the musical and affective part of speech. We can pay avid attention to intonation, given that we can read the words (often quicker than we can hear them).

This means that an image like Figure 6.2 is multi-modal. One mode is the 2D image and its parts. Another mode is the written language. And a third mode is the intonation of the narrator's voice as a sort of verbal soundtrack. There is also a fourth mode, a musical soundtrack. Each of these modes has its own syntax and semantics. Combined together, they also must be assigned meanings (semantic and situated meanings) as a "combined mode" functioning and meaning in its own right. However, for now, we must leave this issue aside.

The narration (done by Danny Wallace) in *TWA* is in a British accent that is amazingly good at indicating the emotions of the characters (rectangles though they be), emotions like fear, self-loathing, loneliness, liking and love, caring, arrogance, humility, and feelings of trust. The fact that the oral narration is mainly there for its intonational (musical) and emotive qualities, and is separated in a way from its words, makes us feel as if the emotions carried by the intonation are inside the characters and palatably feelable inside us as players, as well.

It is as if the narrator is "singing" the emotional lives of the rectangles. All these emotions and attitudes that we attribute to the characters go beyond their literal meanings as, say, "Thomas the average jumper". Now we assign a changing emotional universe to Thomas and the other characters within the different contexts and flow of game play.

We attribute these emotions and attitudes as deeper meanings for each character by considering the contexts they are in. These contexts include the narration as print and as intonation, as well as the different relationships the characters contract with each other in their actions and thoughts and emotions at different points in the game. These are what we called situated meanings.

Consider as an example of how situated (or situating) meaning works in Figure 6.2. Given the words on the screen, the positions of the characters, and the situation we are in in the game at this point, as well as our earlier play in the game, we can attribute to John (the tall yellow rectangle) a meaning or inference like: John wants to help, though not necessarily for altruistic reasons, but because he likes to show off and look good to others.

In a game, this sequence is partly created by the game's designers and partly by what players have done. Let's assume, for the sake of argument, that a screen prior to Figure 6.2 had John, the yellow triangle, down on the same level, as Thomas (the red rectangle) and Chris (the orange square). Assume further the player has jumped

John—a very good jumper—up to where we see him in Figure 6.2, up above Thomas and Chris. From Figure 6.2, as players, we look back to having jumped John up there and we look forward to that fact that we can, if we want, move him to the right, down the little alley, and then again further to the right and away from Thomas and Chris.

In Figure 6.2, the player can readily see, though, that moving John to the right will not get Thomas and Chris up to the ledge so they can move on in the game as well. They cannot alone or together jump high enough to get up to the ledge. John must come back down and allow Chris to jump on top of Thomas and then to jump from Thomas to John and, finally, to jump up to the ledge. Thomas can then jump on John and then up to the ledge. And only then can John jump back up by himself. This creates a sequence in the player's mind, a sequence that he or she can then create and thereby, too, create the actual discourse sequence of the game.

In Figure 6.2 we see that John is higher than Thomas and Chris and that he can easily go on without them. We see, too, that if the game (and its story) is to continue, John must go back down, place himself again on the same level as Thomas and Chris, help them, and then move on last (not first) himself. All these meanings derived from sequence reinforce the sorts of situated meanings we have already drawn from the story and contexts of play.

John thinks more highly of himself than he does of the others. Forced to go back and help, he has to rationalize this as not a weakness, but as a strength. This strength is not only that his help is essential to mitigate Thomas's and Chris's weaknesses. It is also that John will look good in the act and others will see how special he is. All this is meaning or inferences that we as players have derived from the context of the screens as a sequence (or potential sequence) flowing through time.

One powerful element of Figure 6.2, considered within the flow of the game, is that we realize that John realizes he could easily go on without the others. As players we realize that the game is designed in such a way that if we do let John go on, then the game cannot finish, because Thomas and Chris cannot move to the end of the game (which is, for them, a search for freedom from the system they are in). As players we have to rationalize why we must make John go back, beyond being merely forced to do this by the game's design. The rationalization is supplied by the situated meanings we derived from the game's story, changing contexts, and from the flow of the game where John has always gone back and has gotten more pleased with himself as he has (flow and sequence are a larger context than single frames). As is true in many good games, this sort of mixture of player action, game designer's design, game mechanics, and the game's universe is a complex delight.

To a linguist, context includes all the objects and beings present in a situation, all the background knowledge one has and shares with others in the situation, as well as what has come before and what one knows or thinks will come later. Context also includes construals, beliefs, and inferences we make about what is happening in a situation, what is relevant in the situation, and what it all might mean. We can see even in this simple example from *TWA* how important are the ways in which designers and players co-construct context, make decisions about what are the most relevant parts of the context, and about what situated meanings (inferences, interpretations) can be drawn from context.

The situated meaning making work that *TWA* allows us so successfully to do is captured very nicely in a review of the game printed (in part) below:

> Amazingly, I felt more connected to Thomas Was Alone's colored, poly-gonal blocks than I have to most human characters in recent games. Part of the game's genius is how attached you feel to Thomas, John and the other tinted, four-sided personas you encounter in Mike Bithell's indie platformer.
> …
> Blustery narcissism, cranky neediness and occasional jealousy all pop up in the narration pinned to TWA's jumping squares. This game feels like a real investigation into the prickly, soaring thrill ride of actual companionship, complete with people you hang out only because you have to and icky social climbers. …
>
> It's not just the clever writing or great narration by Danny Wallace that won me over. Thomas Was Alone manages to skillfully weave both those elements together with puzzle mechanics that themselves feel like a character arc. As these blobs of suddenly sentient artificial intelligence feel their way around their own personalities, the player's doing the same thing in the gameworld.
>
> *(http://kotaku.com/5929049/thomas-was-alone-the-kotaku-review)*

Conclusion

If discourse analysis can apply to video games and not just language (and we are exploring this possibility without being able to prove it at this point), then why should this be so? There is a reason. The human capacity to understand and interpret language is carried out by the same part of the brain—and in much the same way—as the part that understands and interprets the world (Gee 2004; Stanovich 2000). That is, we comprehend language and the world with the same mental capacities. This is why the famous Brazilian literacy scholar and activist Paulo Freire claimed that "reading the word" and "reading the world" are intimately connected (Freire 1995).

Video games trigger the same capacities by which we understand the world and language. Thus, it would not be surprising that there could be a common theory of meaning making in context (discourse analysis) for language, the world, and games. However, I pointed out earlier that, in language, discourse analysis is related to syntax (to the structure of language) in the sense that syntax determines what is inside a sentence and discourse analysis deals with what the structure and sequence of sentences mean as they are used in specific contexts. We must, thus, develop ideas about what a syntax and semantics might look like for games.

Games are multi-modal. They involve images, words, and sounds. But at a deeper level we should realize that language is already and always has been itself "multi-modal", though this has not often played an overt enough role in linguistic discourse analysis. Spoken language is composed of words and phrases sequenced through time (words and phrases that are themselves composed of structure, meaning, and sound), intonation (pitch, tone, and stress), and embodied postures, gestures, and eye gaze. And, additionally, we can write language and not just speak it. Indeed, *TWA* brings out the multi-modal character of language quite well.

More importantly, while many scholars see discourse (language-in-use sequenced through time) as about information, I would argue that discourse is primarily about action taking (Gee 2004, 2014a). Language-in-use and video games (as well as science and our everyday interactions with the world) are about "discernment of implications for action and response to actions". In verbal interactions and in games, we consider the "system" in front of us in terms of a search for the affordances present so that we can use our effective abilities to act, respond, and reach goals. If we take this perspective, as I think we should, then we may have as much or more to learn about discourse analysis from games as we have to learn about games from discourse analysis.

7

AN INTERIM SUMMARY

Introduction

This chapter just repeats in somewhat different words—and in a rather philosophical way—ideas we have already gone over in this book. I repeat them here because for some readers these ideas may be counter-intuitive. Perhaps, saying them all together and in a somewhat different way will help some readers. Readers who feel comfortable with the ideas in this book so far—or who do not find this chapter helpful—can skip this chapter.

Language

What is a language?

A language is any set of symbols that stand for or refer to objects or relationships. The set of symbols must have basic symbols that can combine by rules into combinations of symbols.

The rules by which basic symbols combine into combinations are called syntactic rules.

In natural languages like English and Mandarin, the basic units are "words". There are syntactic rules in each language in terms of which words can combine into acceptable ("grammatical") phrases and phrases into clauses and sentences. For example, in English the word "red" (an adjective) can combine with the world "flower" (a noun) to create the phrase "red flower" (a noun phrase). Words are basic units and phrases are combinations of words.

A language must also, in addition to syntactic rules, have a semantics. Semantics assigns each basic symbol a meaning in the sense of a thing or relationship in the world it names, refers to, or stands for.

Semantics also states what combinations of basic symbols mean in terms of how the meanings of the meanings of basic units of which they are composed can be combined. Thus, in English "red flower" means something that is both red and a flower, while "small elephant" does not mean something that is small and an elephant, but something that is small for an elephant.

Semantics assigns meanings to words and phrases based on a "universe of discourse". A universe of discourse is a set of things and relationships among them that exist in a given world, domain of reality, or area of belief.

We can treat any set of symbols with basic units and rules by which they can combine (a syntax) and an interpretation in terms of what the symbols stand for or refer to (semantics) as a language.

A language, thus, requires: symbols, basic symbols, rules for combining basic symbols into larger combinations (syntax), a universe of discourse (the set of things and relationships the basic units and larger units can stand for or refer to), and a set of rules that assign each basic unit and combination of units a meaning in terms of what is in the universe of discourse (semantics).

English is, of course, along with Spanish and Mandarin, a language in this sense. So are branches of mathematics like algebra, geometry, and calculus.

Human "natural languages" like English and Mandarin can be spoken or written. Some languages (e.g., programming languages) can only be written, not spoken. And, of course, there have been many human natural languages that have never been written down.

We have a special word for decoding and understanding written language: "reading". Oddly, perhaps, we have no word for decoding and understanding oral language. This is probably because, in the case of human natural languages, learning to read is a more arduous and overt process than learning to listen, and reading seems more effortful to many humans than does listening.

Academics sometimes use the word "text" to mean any stretch or body of written language. Again, we have no word for stretches or blocks of spoken language. Often, academics will use the word "text" for both written and oral language, a usage that offends everyday ways of speaking, since in everyday language we take the word "text" to refer only to written language.

When people read written texts, they have to decode (in their heads) the symbols (letters) and strings of symbols into meaningful words and phrases. This is what we call "reading". But it is also true that when people hear oral language they have to decode (in their heads) its symbols (sounds) and sequences of sounds into meaningful words and phrases. The processes of decoding oral language and written language are not wholly the same, but, nonetheless, they are both in a sense a type of "reading".

Worlds

So far we have defined what a language is. We have also said that when we decode and understand either written symbols or spoken ones we are doing a type of "reading".

Now we are going to take up the question: What is the world? What is reality? Interestingly enough, some religions (e.g., early Christianity) and mythologies (e.g., Dreamtime stories among some Australian Aborigines) consider the world as a "text" written by God, gods, or spirits, a text that can be "read".

I will argue here that for humans the world is a "text" that we "read" and, in that sense, we treat the world as if it was written in a language. However, we need not believe that God wrote the world in order to be able to read it.

In one sense, the real world is just what is "out there". It is the "stuff" that we see, sense, feel, and sometimes get hurt by. However, we humans have no direct access to the world. We must see it with our human senses. Our human senses sense the world differently—for example, see different colors—than do the senses of other animals.

Our human eyes, thanks to evolution, see the world in a certain way. Other animals (e.g., bees, cats, octopuses, bats) have different sorts of eyes and brains than we do and so they see the world differently than we do. For example, bees see colors we do not and dogs hear sounds we do not.

What is real? The colors we see and the sounds we hear, or the ones bees see or dogs hear? This is a question that has no answer, since no organism can see "all" that is the world, that is, see the world in all possible ways.

Scientists have special tools that supplement the human eye. For example, they can see cells and chromosomes thanks to electron microscopes. We cannot see these with our eyes unaided by such a tool. Science has taught modern people that not everything that exists is open to our unaided senses. We humans see more of what is real the more tools we design, but there is no way to know whether and if we will ever "see" it all and know everything that exists.

Humans do not just move around in the world. They seek to understand it. Indeed, a failure to understand it can lead to injury and death. The real world as we humans interact with it—not as it is in of itself to some God like creature—has a syntax just like a language does.

That syntax is determined by how a creature's eye and brain works. For unaided human vision the world is made up of basic units like colors, spaces, and lines. The initial image on our retinas is two-dimensional, upside down, and composed only of lines, angles, and vaguely bounded shapes and spaces.

These basic units are combined by the eye and brain into well bounded objects. We can see three lines as composing a triangle or a set of lines and spaces as composing a three-dimensional block. The eye and brain working together impose a syntax on the world, combining basic units into combinations and larger patterns. Of course, we are no more conscious of this process than we are of the process of combining words into phrases when we speak or listen.

The objects and patterns the eye and brain impose on the world do not have any meaning until we give them meaning with a semantics. Our brains associate given objects and shapes with culturally meaningful identities. The tall tube with wavy shapes at the top is a "tree" (to some cultures). The slinky tube on a flat surface is a snake moving on the ground. The world does not come with "red cardinals" (birds). It has red cardinals in it only for creatures who can see red and have the cultural categories of birds, species, and cardinals.

Our minds have a universe of discourse that defines for us—given our culture—what exists in the world. We assign things and relationships from this universe of discourse to shapes, patterns, and objects that our eyes (and other sense organs) and brains have composed from sensations we have received from the physical world.

This is to say that we treat the world as a sort of language. We see it in terms of basic units and their combinations into larger patterns. We assign meanings to these units and patterns based on what we assume exists in the world, based on our cultural knowledge.

Different animals see in different ways. Different cultures assume different sorts of things exist. So there is no one real world. There are many, differing by the sense organs that construe the world and the meanings an animal or a human cultural or social group assign to it.

So we treat the world as written in a meaningful language we can "read" (with our eyes and brains). Of course we can use verbal language (like English) to talk about the world. When we do so, it is somewhat like we are translating back and forth from one language (the world as we see and interpret it) to another (e.g., English).

So, though we do not use the word "read" this way in everyday life, we can say that we humans can read oral language, written language, and the world. Indeed, different sorts of humans, based on different cultures and different access to science, read each of them differently.

Some scientists "see" (with their special tools) atoms as the basic units and molecules, proteins, and bodies as combinations thereof. Most of us see color and shapes as basic units and bounded objects as combinations of these. A chair is made up of shapes (a back, seat, legs) and a color or colors, not atoms and molecules for most of us.

Non-real worlds

We have just seen that there is a plurality of real worlds. We humans read the world in different ways depending upon our cultures and our tools. But we humans are also adept at creating "non-real" worlds, worlds that are different in some respect from the real world. These are worlds like mythology, science fiction, religion, and baseball (where "strikes" exist not as physically real, but as conventions of the game; if there was no baseball there would be no strikes).

Each of these non-real worlds is treated as having basic units and combinations of basic units (e.g., in some mythological worlds you can combine a horn and a horse or a horse and wings). Furthermore, these basic units and their combinations are assigned meaning within the mythological universe of discourse (e.g., horse with horn = unicorn, an animal only visible to virgins). So we treat non-real worlds like mythology as language like too. They have patterns and meanings we can "read" and "understand" and "translate".

Saying a world is "non-real" does not mean it is considered inferior by a given culture or group. It might in fact be considered special and more important.

Humans are adept at creating worlds (like religions, mythology, science fiction, video game worlds, conventional sports, and so forth). And these worlds are treated as forms of meaningful language, as giving rise to "texts" we can "read" (decode and understand). They are treated as having basic units and patterns of basic units that refer to or stand for things and relationships that are in one of our human universes of discourse.

Video games

Video games are virtual worlds. Games designers design a world that is, like all worlds for us humans, readable like a text. Players read the game world. Indeed, if they cannot, they cannot play the game. If they cannot read it well, they cannot win the game.

Since a game world is visual, at one level it has the same grammar (syntax and semantics) as the real world. Players do have to read the game in visual terms of course.

However, because game worlds are designed as problem-solving spaces, they also have a different grammar, what we can call a "game world grammar".

In game worlds, the basic units are objects (like a box) and the objects can combine in certain ways (e.g., box-on-ledge). These objects and their combinations are seeable thanks to how human vision works, they are the result of lots of visual processing. Games use the outcome of this visual processing as the starting point for designing a new kind of world and a new world language.

The semantics of a game world is what makes it special. Things in a game are interpreted not just in terms of what they are (what cultural category they fall into). They are interpreted as well in terms of what they are good for, that is, in terms of what affordances they have for action. A crate is interpreted in some games as "breakable object". A tube filled with blue liquid is interpreted as a "power up" (probably some form of mana). The combination of crate, weapon, and blue tube can be interpreted as "break crate with weapon to get mana power up".

Game designers take the syntax and semantics of the real world (or some other visual world) and make on top of it another syntax and semantics. This game syntax and semantics is based on actions and affordances for action to solve specific sorts of problems. The universe of discourse for a game contains the things that exist in the game world labeled in terms of what they are good for. Corridors do not just exist in *Metal Gear Solid*, they are "escape routes", among other things. Guards are not primarily humans, they are dangerous obstacles that need to be gotten around.

Now of course, this game world perspective is a stance we humans can and do take towards the real world when we have goals and need to take actions to accomplish them. Then too we see the world in terms of what things are good for, in terms of affordances for actions.

But there is a difference. The real world was built by evolution and is infinitely more complex than any game world. In fact, games and game worlds are engaging to humans in large part because they allow us to "play" with a stance we need often to take to the real world, but play with this stance under much more controlled, predictable, and safe conditions. In the real world, an action and affordance stance is often necessary for survival, but rarely results in clear win states, or least, not in ones that are permanent.

Conversations

We can view talk as verbal action. We do not just say things when we talk, we do things. For example, we seek to inform, convince, motivate, and manipulate others through our words. Furthermore, the other can talk back, respond, and act on us. It is a two-way street.

When we act in and on the real world, we do things not with words but with actions. We seek to manipulate the world in some way. The world "talks back" and responds to our actions in ways that are good or bad for our purposes and goals. This is what we have called a conversation with the world. So we humans don't just read the real world, but we talk to it, converse with it, as well.

There are some worlds that we can read but cannot talk to, cannot act in and on. The world of mythology is one such world. We can read images like a horned horse accompanied by a virgin as a "unicorn". But the world of mythology will not respond back to our readings, because we cannot act in it. That is part of what it means to say it is non-real.

Video games, however, are non-real worlds that can respond. We can act in and on them and get back responses that guide further action. We can have conversations with video game worlds. The real world and video game worlds, then, are both like written language in that we can read them and like oral language in that we can talk to them and get a response. We talk to the real world and video game worlds through action. But, remember, oral language is a form of action as well, actions we do to other people. All conversations (with other people, with the world, and with games) are actions and responses to actions (or happenings).

8

A UNIFIED THEORY OF DISCOURSE ANALYSIS

A framework for discourse analysis

We now have a framework for discourse analysis that applies to verbal conversations, conversations with world, and conversations with video games. The framework can be stated as a set of questions that the discourse analyst can ask. The questions below do not have to be asked in any specific order. Furthermore, even though I use singular nouns below, there can be more than one syntax, semantics, universe of discourse, conversation, and so forth going on in a piece of data:

1   Who or what are the conversational partners? What histories and complexities do they bring to the encounter?
2   How does syntax work? What are the basic units and how do they combine?
3   How does semantics work?
    a) What universe of discourse is involved?
    b) How was the universe of discourse determined?
    c) How are meanings assigned from the universe of discourse?
4   What is the avatar?
    a) How does the avatar function as an identity?
    b) How does the avatar function as a surrogate body?
    c) How does the avatar function as a tool-kit?
5   How are affordances and effective abilities aligned?
6   How does X-ray vision function?
    a) What are the relevant details for aligning affordances and effective abilities?
    b) What tools are being used to supplement "seeing" and interaction?
7   How is meaning being situated? How are situated meanings being created?
    a) What is the context? How is it being construed and constructed?
    b) What are the relevant aspects of the context and how is relevance being determined?

c) How is "packaging"—how units are combined (syntax)—helping to create situated meaning? What were alternative ways things could have been packaged? What does it mean that these alternatives were not used?

d) How does the sequence and flow of sentences, utterances, or activities work to help create situated meanings?

e) What style or social language is being used? How does its units and their combinations (its distinctive syntax and semantics) function to carry out distinctive tasks or work for which it was invented?

8 What is the role of story (top-down, authored stories or stories produced in the course of interaction); cultural, social, scientific, or other sorts of theories, models, schemas, or frames; and beliefs, values, and ideologies?

9 How is a "player's story" being constructed by the choices, decisions, actions, interactions, successes and failures the "player" experiences as he or she talks, acts, and plays? (Here I use "player" for anyone speaking, writing, acting on the world, or playing a game.)

This framework is meant to apply to talk in interaction and interactions with worlds and video games (which are, of course, types of worlds). We have argued earlier that when we converse with another person, we treat that person as a world in and on which we act. So in this framework all conversations are conversations between people and worlds.

An example

Let's take a simple example to see how the framework works. Below is a small piece of data from a classroom (data from Mruczek 2012). A teacher is teaching reading to young children:

Teacher: … Ready? The next word is … (three second pause) right.
            Please turn right.
            Right. (Pause)
            Ok.
            How do you spell right?
            Everyone?
Students and teacher (many of them, in unison):   R … i … g … h … t.
Teacher: Right.
            You got it.
            Let's sound it out, ready?

Who or what are the conversational partners? What histories and complexities do they bring to the encounter?

The conversational partners are a teacher and young students. Teachers and students behave in different ways in different schools, within different practices, and at different times in history. Being a teacher of a certain sort or being a student of a certain sort are social identities or avatars. Today, there are all sorts of controversies around teachers, students, schools, and school reform which might be relevant to an analysis.

How does syntax work? What are the basic units and how do they combine?

The syntax here is the grammar of English as it functions in "teacher talk". Teacher talk is a style of language (a social language) used in schools to carry out the purposes and tasks of formal schooling in certain ways. There are, of course, different styles of teacher talk based on what type of a teacher a teacher is trying to be. Teacher talk can vary by schools, practices, and across history. Nonetheless, we and the students recognize teacher talk and the appropriate styles of language students are intended to use in talking to the teacher.

How does semantics work?

What universe of discourse is involved?

Of course, the teacher and students probably have a largely overlapping universe of discourse for the real world. But they also each have an overlapping universe of discourse for what exists in school as its own special world or domain. This universe of discourse includes things like desks, tests, grades, drill-sheets, report cards, homework, and routine practices (like the one in our data, namely "IRE", which is a pattern of Initiation by the teacher, Reply by students, and Evaluation by teacher of the student response), and so forth. Different sorts of classrooms operate with different universes of discourse (and we may soon see some with no human teachers, but just students and machines).

How was the universe of discourse determined?

This universe of discourse is determined by the history of schooling and by public policies and shared cultural and social norms about schooling. It is also contentious at the present moment thanks to controversies about schools and school reform. Some people would like to significantly change the universe of discourse of schooling and classrooms.

How are meanings assigned from the universe of discourse?

It is an easy matter for students to assign the thing they are sitting at the identity as a "desk". However, it is trickier to know how to identify the teacher's question about spelling. Is this a "test", "a known-answer question", "a scripted lesson starter", "a genuine question", "a move in a ritual" or some or all of the above? The answer depends on how clear the operative universe of discourse has been made for the students. It is not uncommon for teachers and students to be operating with different meanings and interpretations without knowing it consciously or realizing it.

What is the avatar?

How does the avatar function as an identity?

The teacher is talking and acting out of the identity of a teacher of a certain sort. The students are talking and acting out of identities of students of certain sorts. There are, of course, today controversies about how teachers and students ought to act and interact and how much these identities should be controlled by publishers, testers, and policy makers. We would need more data to better characterize the teacher's social identity—the avatar she is "playing"—but it might well be a traditional skill-and-drill teacher following curriculum and policies that have come from "above" as mandates.

How does the avatar function as a surrogate body?

Teachers are expected, in this sort of classroom world and in this sort of activity, to stand in front of the students as a whole group. Students are expected to sit up, speak when spoken to, and show attention on their faces and bodies. They are expected to space their bodies away from each other in the appropriate way and focus on the teacher not their classmates. Teachers are supposed to monitor the bodies and gazes of the students. In a very different classroom I once visited, the teacher played her role of teacher more like a coach. The students lounged around her as she overviewed how the day would go, where they would have choices to make, and what the expectations would be. After this "pep talk" type of session, the students operated in groups and as individuals pretty much on their own steam, asking for help or getting it from the "coach"/teacher when they needed it. Teacher and students moved freely around the room and arranged and re-arranged themselves in terms of tasks that needed to get done.

How does the avatar function as a tool-kit?

The teacher has curriculum guides and she has the power to control, give orders, reward, and punish. The students have textbooks and drill-sheets and most of them have the necessary skills and willingness to answer known-answer questions, display for the teacher, and follow her instructions. Those who do not have these skills get to play a different avatar, namely "problem student" or "at risk student". Some of these tools were produced by publishers and/or mandated by policy makers.

How are affordances and effective abilities aligned?

Students look for what can be used, given their abilities, to display competence to the teacher. They see the question about spelling as an opportunity to display knowledge if they have the ability to spell. If they do not have the ability to spell, they will see this as an opportunity to fail and not as something that affords them the opportunity to impress the teacher. Some students might see the request to turn right as an affordance to go overboard and push the limits on how ebulliently they are supposed to use their bodies in a classroom and some will have the effective abilities and the will to use these affordances. Those students who are enacting the avatar "problem student" (by choice or circumstance) may see this as a good opportunity. One interesting thing in classrooms, is that different students may see the available affordances differently and may have different effective abilities (and willingness) to use them. They may even see the "game" they are playing differently. In many classrooms students too often fail to proactively look for and take up affordances for learning rather than for display, grades, or getting by.

How does X-ray vision function?

Students know that they must "see through" a politeness marker like "please" in "Please turn right" to see it as merely honorific. What is really relevant for action about "Please turn right" is the command, not the politeness. In general, students need to see details that are relevant to display as important and background other details. In this activity, the teacher may see through the students as complex human beings to see details relevant to assessment about phonics, learning to read, and "good behavior". In some schools, learning is subordinated to assessment.

What are the relevant details for aligning affordances and effective abilities alignment?

For the teacher a student's posture and focus of attention are relevant details for assessing whether the student is a "good student" or a "problem student". For students, the teacher's "Right. Got it" is relevant as a type of evaluation that says they have succeeded and are ready to go on to the next part of the "script", namely sounding out the letters in the word they have just spelled.

What tools are being used to supplement "seeing" and interaction?

The teacher may well have teacher guides and assessment guides that shape how she sees students and what they do. The students may have textbooks and drill-sheets that shape how they see what they are doing and how the teacher is behaving. The classroom walls may be full of images and posters some of which shape how students see the teacher, the classroom, each other, and what they are doing. They have no special tools that would allow them to see how sounds work in language (i.e., that we humans cannot hear the individual sounds in words, since they are smudged together and, thus, it is hard to learn how to line them up one-by-one with letters, harder for some children than for others).

How is meaning being situated? How are situated meanings created?

What is the context? How is it being construed and constructed?

The context is a phonics (matching sounds and letters) activity that follows a clear and practiced routine. The students construe the context as a reading lesson in which they may be being tacitly assessed. They help actually construct the context as a choral form of large-group scripted display by their actions and willingness to follow along (if they are so willing—otherwise they might construe and construct the context as a time and place to act out or get recognized as a failure).

What are the relevant aspects of the context and how is relevance being determined?

The desks, walls, posters, and drill-sheets, as well as the question-answer-evaluation (IRE) format of the talk are relevant aspects of the context. The teacher's weight and the students' emotional states (if they are not displayed as a disruption) are not relevant parts of the context. What is and is not relevant in the context is determined by often taken-for-granted cultural values, institutional forces, and long repetition of such activities and such classrooms. The teacher and the students are following conventions that they may or may not have ever questioned. It is also possible that a curriculum maker or policy maker is helping to determine what counts as relevant.

How is "packaging"—how units are combined (syntax)—helping to create situated meaning? What were alternative ways things could have been packaged? What does it mean that these alternatives were not used?

"Please turn right" is packaged as a polite request. Had it been said as "Turn right" its true identity as a command would have been too overtly apparent (especially in the sorts of middle-class cultures that mask authority). "Right. Got it" is packaged as an evaluation ("right") and an assessment that learning has taken place and we can move on ("Got it"). If the teacher had said "Correct. Got it" she would have missed the opportunity to use the word "right" again. Since the teacher spells the word out loud in unison with some of the students, she did not need to say "Right. Got it" at all. She could just have moved on to sounding out the word. In this case, the students would have seen her question about how to spell the world as a question she was answering herself or was telling the students the answer to. However, then the students would not have felt rewarded or validated. *What does it mean that these alternatives were not used?* (This is always an important question: what is not said is often as important as what is said.) What it means in part is that the teacher wants to mask authority and the routine nature of what they are doing and "pretend" it is a normal, engaging, informal interaction between an adult and children.

How does the sequence and flow of sentences, utterances, or activities work to help create situated meanings?

The sequence "question-answer-evaluation" that we see here is a classic routine in school. It is sometimes called the I-R-E sequence (Initiation-Reply-Evaluation). It is a routine that "mimics" conversation, dialogue, and discussion when it is actually a form of teaching by testing. It is a hallmark of traditional schooling and part of what allows the teacher, the students, and us as analysts to identify what is going on here as traditional schooling, in this case a phonics lesson.

What style or social language is being used? How does its units and their combinations (its distinctive syntax and semantics) function to carry out distinctive tasks or work for which it was invented?

One style of language or social language at play here is "teacher talk" of a certain sort. Here language forms are recruited for the giving of polite orders, engaging in script like routines, assessing, and in controlling children's actions and responses.

What is the role of story (top-down, authored stories or stories produced in the course of interaction); cultural, social, scientific, or other sorts of theories, models, schemas, or frames; and beliefs, values, and ideologies?

Nearly everyone in the United States has gone to school. So people have ideas (a theory or model) of how school "should" work. They have stories they tell themselves and others about their schools and schooling. They may have ideologies (value-oriented beliefs) in which school should be about teacher control, basic skills, learning to follow instructions, and getting prepared to get a job after school. Teachers, students, and families are influenced by these stories, theories, values, and ideologies. There are also formal theories promulgated by curriculum designers, educational professors, publishers, and policy makers that influence teachers, students, and families. Then, of course, each teacher and student has his or her own story of the decisions they have made and the actions and interactions they have had in this classroom and in classrooms before.

How is a "player's story" being constructed by the choices, decisions, actions, interactions, successes and failures the "player" experiences as he or she talks, acts, and plays? (Here I use "player" for anyone speaking, writing, acting on the world, or playing a game.)

The teacher and each of the children in this class experience this as one episode in their stories or histories as a teacher and as students in school. How they relate this episode across time becomes an integral part of their own story and, thus, too the significance of parts of their lives. A teacher could see this as an exercise she chose and supports or as one imposed on her by others. Students could see this as a fun activity where they get to display knowledge, practice, and learn. Or they could see it as boring, rote, and too decontextualized from what they find meaningful. It could be part of a chain of successes for one child and part of a chain of losses for another. There are, of course, a number of other ways the teacher and students could fit this episode into their ongoing stories as a teacher and students.

The example above is not, of course, a full analysis or even very meaningful as it stands alone. It is just meant to show how the framework can surface questions or issues that could be the beginning points of a fuller discourse analysis.

None of the remarks above mean that what is going on in the classroom is "bad" or "good". Such a judgment would require much more analysis of data and a statement of how we would evaluate such judgments (i.e., on what basis, value system, or theory). Nonetheless, with even the few remarks we have made above we can see that the teacher and students are having a conversation (verbal responsive interaction) that is routine and caught up with ideas about traditional schooling. These ideas about traditional schooling are ones many of us recognize and have experienced, but ideas about schooling that are, nonetheless, controversial today in certain ways due to discussions about school reform and arguments between "liberals" and "conservatives".

All schooling of young children is about socializing them into what it means to be a student of a certain sort (a type of avatar) and into what it means to be educated and literate. But such socializing can take different forms and can be a point of conflict, controversy, and contestation. Some classrooms use games to practice phonics, others embed phonics instruction inside reading literature, others memorize phonics rules. (By the way, this teacher realizes that spelling and phonics are closely connected. People who are good at associating sounds and letters are usually good spellers and good spellers are usually good at associating sounds and letters.)

Another example

Let's briefly discuss a related piece of data that can bring us closer to seeing how we can direct discourse analysis towards a concrete point relevant to an important issue. The data below involves a second grade teacher teaching reading (Gee 2014b).

The teacher is working with a small group of students. She first dictates a sentence that the students have to write down. The sentence was "I love the puppy". Then she dictates a list of words, one at a time, which the children are to write down with correct spelling. After they have finished the list, the teacher asks the children how the word "love" in the original sentence and each word on the list, one after the other, is spelled. The children are supposed to correct each spelling, if they have made a mistake, after the teacher has elicited the correct spelling orally from the children.

This is another reading/spelling/phonics lesson. The teacher is trying to show the students that there is a family of words that display a spelling and sound pattern. In words like "love", "shove", "dove", "come", "none", and others, the vowel spelled with an "o" is said as a short "u" sound ("uh") when followed by a consonant plus "silent e". This pattern is interesting in that it violates a larger pattern in which many vowels in English are pronounced by a long vowel sound when they are followed by a consonant plus "silent e": e.g., "line", "tone", "late", "fume", and many more.

The teacher is showing the students that there are patterns even amidst what seem exceptions. She is showing them that English spelling and the way we decode letters into sound is more regular than we often think. This is all to the good, because we do not want young readers to think that spelling and decoding letters into sounds is completely chaotic or unpredictable.

Below is what one African-American girl's list looked like. Note that "sume" ("some") and "shuve" ("shove") are spelled incorrectly:

dove
sume
glove
one
shuve
come
none

As we said, the teacher has the children correct the original sentence and then each word in the list one-by-one, eliciting the correct spelling for each one. When she gets to "some", the second word on the list, the African-American girl corrects it, then notices what the pattern is and goes ahead and corrects "shuve" further down the list. The teacher stops her and sharply reprimands her, saying that they have to go "one at a time" and she shouldn't "go ahead".

The teacher moves on to have the small group of children engage in a "picture walk" of a book. This is an activity where children "read the pictures" in a book, using each picture in turn to predict what the text in the book will say. The African-American girl bounces in her chair repeatedly, enthusiastically volunteering for each picture. The teacher tells her to calm down. The girl says, "I'm sorry, but I'm so happy?". The teacher responds, "Well, just calm down".

Now in this data we begin to see how our framework can work in an illuminating way. Here we are seeing how children in school learn new avatars (identities) and how to "play them" in the "game" of schooling of a certain sort.

Who or what are the conversational partners? What histories and complexities do they bring to the encounter?

The conversational partners are a teacher and young students, as in our previous example. In this example, we have given two interactions between a middle-aged Anglo-American teacher and a young African-American girl who is working in a small group with the teacher.

How does syntax work? What are the basic units and how are they combined?

Again, we have the language of "teacher talk" of a certain sort centered around a routine activity and instructions and corrections. In this case, the teacher is using directives that are not masked with politeness (as in our example above).

How does semantics work?

What universe of discourse is involved?

The African-American girl is learning what is and what is not in the universe of discourse of this type of schooling. Her body and emotions should exist only in certain ways, with not too much ebullience in body or emotion. As a personal being with her own level of excitement and outside of school emotions, she does not really exist in this activity and, perhaps, this classroom.

How was the universe of discourse determined?

Here we see it actually being shaped. When the girl is told to "calm down" and her statement that she is "so happy" elicits no response (as it surely would have outside school), she is learning what sort of avatar she is meant to be in this activity and that some of her emotions and ways of being outside of school don't exist here or should not be displayed here.

How are meanings assigned from the universe of discourse?

The girl might have thought that going ahead and correcting her errors showed she had learned the pattern and the point of the lesson. Since she was reprimanded this must not have been the real (or only) point of the lesson. She is learning not to assign her excitement, body, and emotions as meaningfully existent things in this classroom, at least for activities like this. She is, in turn, learning that such ebullience and emotions exist here only as negative things, things to be eradicated.

What is the avatar?

How does the avatar function as an identity?

The teacher is talking and acting out of the identity of a teacher of a certain sort. The girl is learning that she is playing the wrong avatar and needs to play another one. The "right" avatar does not show too much excitement, does not "go ahead", diligently follows instructions, and suppresses emotions that are not "relevant" to the activity as a school-based reading lesson.

How does the avatar function as a surrogate body?

The girl is learning to restrain her body and its expression of emotions. She is learning what "surrogate body" she is supposed to have in school.

How does the avatar function as a tool-kit?

The girl has a sheet of paper ruled for a sample sentence and a list of slots for the spelling words. It looks like a tool just for learning to spell, but it is in fact also a tool for learning how to follow instructions and delay gratification (even the gratification you have seen the point of the lesson).

How are affordances and effective abilities aligned?

The girl "misread" the affordances in the situation. She thought the activity in the spelling lesson afforded the opportunity to "go ahead, once you saw the pattern". She thought that the "picture walk" afforded the opportunity for excitement and putting your body and soul into the activity. Neither of these things were true. She was supposed to be showing or developing the effective ability to follow instructions, go sequentially, and stay calm and "low pitched".

How does X-ray vision function?

The little girl had not yet developed the right way to see. But the lesson is teaching her how to see what details are relevant for the actual goals of the lesson. She is learning that what is relevant in this context is details that allow students to display not just knowledge, but also to display the "right" behavior, emotional control, and body. She "should" have seen that what was really relevant about the drill-sheet was that the words were in a sequential order so they could be "corrected" one after the other. She should have seen that what was relevant about the pictures in the book was not how much you enjoyed them, but how they gave you an opportunity to take turns in a quiet and well-ordered way.

What are the relevant details for aligning affordances and effective abilities?

For the teacher the girl's body and emotions are relevant details for assessing whether she is "behaving" as she "should" in a reading lesson. The girl mistakenly thought the teacher's humanity and caring as teacher was an affordance for getting a personal response to her emotions and enthusiasm. She thought that excitement was a relevant detail that would afford the teacher the opportunity to see her as a "good" and "motivated" student. She thought "going ahead" in the spelling lesson was not "cheating" but showing the teacher she got the point and had learned. She is learning otherwise. She is learning that the relevant details for alignment here are the ones that let you show you can follow instructions and maintain "control" (which here means low pitch, low ebullience).

What tools are being used to supplement "seeing" and interaction?

The student has no tools to know what was the "right" way to see and interact (play her avatar). Schools rarely tell students such things overtly. They assume children have learned how to "do school" at home or will "catch on" through corrections from the teacher, corrections that rarely explain why the "rules" are as they are.

How is meaning being situated? How are situated meanings created?

What is the context? How is it being construed and constructed?

The context is a multi-part reading lesson that follows routines that are clear and well-practiced for some of the students and not for others. The students here need to construe the context as a reading lesson in which they are not just being taught reading but being taught control of a certain sort. They are being taught what bodies and identities their avatars are supposed to have in this context.

What are the relevant aspects of the context and how is relevance being determined?

Some of the relevant aspects are sequence, linear order, taking turns, following instructions, and being quiet. Ironically, perhaps, knowing the pattern being taught or feeling excitement over participating are not relevant parts of the context unless they are displayed in the "right" way. The fact that the teacher seems like or even is a "friend" or "care-giver" is not a relevant part of the context in this sort of lesson. *How is relevance being determined?* The little girl is applying a theory or cultural framework about school that is "wrong" here. Her idea is that teachers are care-givers, parent-like beings who will respond to you as a child in terms of your home-based identity, ways of being, body and emotions. While this may or may not be true of other activities in this classroom, it is not true in this one. Research has shown that some cultural groups do not want to learn from teachers who do not value them as "who they are" in their community and home-based identities. Other groups are willing to learn from teachers even if they feel these teachers do not value or even look down on their community and home-based identities.

How is "packaging"—how units are combined (syntax)—helping to create situated meaning? What were alternative ways things could have been packaged? What does it mean that these alternatives were not used?

In many contexts in the world when someone says "I'm so happy", the appropriate response is something like "Great" or "Why?". The teacher could have said one of these, but instead she said "Calm down". When the student went "ahead" on the spelling list, the teacher could have said "Great, you got it!", but instead she said the girl should not "go ahead". These choices create a context in which students should situate following instructions, going in order, and being calm and quiet with a controlled body as the meanings of this lesson, just as much as or more than learning to read. *What does it mean that these alternatives were not used?* Here, unlike our first example, the teacher is not masking authority, but overtly displaying it. She is not using politeness forms and she is not responding as a "friend" or an adult who cares about why you are happy or how excited you are about "reading" pictures. That the alternatives were not used should mean to the children that this is an encounter between teacher-as-controller engaged in "best practice" and students as well-controlled reading students following instructions correctly. Here the students should not confuse the teacher as "someone who cares" other than "professionally". Now, of course, this may or may not be true of other sorts of activities in this classroom or school.

How does the sequence and flow of sentences, utterances, or activities work to help create situated meanings?

Here sequence helps create the meaning that "going in order" and quietly taking turns is important. Ironically, perhaps, sequence here is "the point" in several different ways: do not go ahead, do not go overboard, do not get out of control, be well ordered.

What style or social language is being used? How does its units and their combinations (its distinctive syntax and semantics) function to carry out distinctive tasks or work for which it was invented?

The teacher is using directives or orders that are not softened or mitigated in any way. She is using a style of language that has been found to be more typical of working-class homes than upper-middle-class ones, where directives are often replaced by explanations and negotiations that allow children the opportunity to engage in more extended talk with adults. Of course, this is teacher talk in school and not parent talk at home. Nonetheless, not all teachers use directives in this way, though many teachers may see it as important in order to keep order and save time.

What is the role of story (top-down, authored stories or stories produced in the course of interaction); cultural, social, scientific, or other sorts of theories, models, schemas, or frames; and beliefs, values, and ideologies?

This data comes from a study where we concluded that teachers in this school—like teachers in some of the other schools in this town—operated by a model, theory, or story that if you gave certain types of children (especially minority children) an "inch", they will take a "mile". Even a small amount of ebullience or "lack of control" would spiral out of control if not stopped "in its tracks". It was also the case that teachers in this town took a low-pitch, toned-down, calm and quiet persona as the norm for people, especially in school. They therefore often took excitement or noise to mean disruption even when they seemed to us "outsiders" to mean engagement and involved learning. The girl is bringing her own community and home-based cultural norms, frame, theories, and values to school and learning they do not match well with the frames, theories, values, and ideologies of the school.

How is a "player's story" being constructed by the choices, decisions, actions, interactions, successes and failures the "player" experiences as he or she talks, acts, and plays? (Here I use "player" for anyone speaking, writing, acting on the world, or playing a game)

This episode could, over time, mean many different things to the student, depending on how she comes to see it as part of her own developing story as a student. Perhaps, it will play a pivotal role as an event that taught her to "divide" herself from school, keeping aspects of her own individuality and culture from integrating with her identity as a student, rather than using them as sources of motivation and creativity for that identity. Perhaps this episode will shape the type of avatar she sees schooling as demanding and, thus, too, the sort of "game" she comes to see school as.

This analysis has more "bite" than the earlier one, because it bears on even more controversial cultural, social, and political issues. The analysis—partial as it is—clearly raises an important question about the "correct" balance between control or regulation and learning and motivation in school. Can control or regulation send messages that sometimes undermine the teacher's learning goals for students? Does this happen more for some sorts of students than others? Can teachers "ruin" the "game" of school for some sorts of children? Should teachers and schools do a better job of overtly explaining the rules of the "game" and the nature of the "avatar" in school practices? Should we change the game and its avatars for teachers and students?

9

CHIBI-ROBO

A video game example

We turn now to an example of our unified discourse framework applied to a commercial video game. The game is the first *Chibi-Robo*. *Chibi-Robo* is a Japanese game that was played across the world. It is an innovative game and like all such games did not please all players. I found it one of the best and most engaging games I have ever played (and I have played hundreds by now).

Below I reprint a screen shot from *Chibi-Robo* (see Figure 9.1).

Who or what are the conversational partners? What histories and complexities do they bring to the encounter?

The conversational partners are the player and the game. Players have their own distinctive identities and histories as gamers. There are many different types of games each with their own histories as forms of media and their own conventions. Both of these types of diversity can be part of a discourse analysis devoted to actual play sessions. This game was controversial. Some players (like me) loved it and others found it tedious. Some liked the colorful cartoon graphics, others found them "out of date". Obviously different sorts of players brought quite different expectations to the game.

Chibi-Robo is a game made in Japan. Japanese games are often quite different than games made in the United States. Gamers are aware of this and many Japanese games—like Japanese anime—have become popular across the world. As is more common in Japanese than American games, *Chibi-Robo* is a game that simulates a real-world activity in a colorful fantasy world. The game also deals with themes that are common in Japanese games, themes like what makes something human and family and environmental issues (Napier 2005).

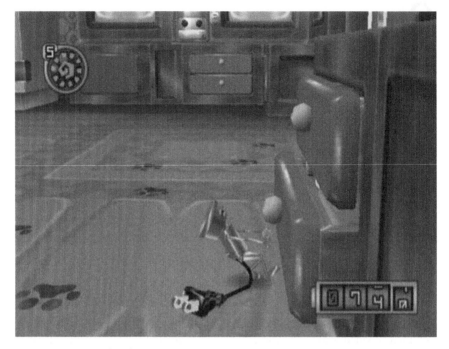

FIGURE 9.1 Screenshot from *Chibi-Robo*

Chibi-Robo is a four-inch house-cleaning robot who earns "Happy Points" by cleaning house and otherwise making the family he works for happy. He was bought as a toy by the father in the family for his daughter. The family Chibi is helping is dysfunctional because the parents are constantly fighting about money and the daughter is traumatized by it all. In fact, she wears a frog suit and will only say "Ribbit". In addition to cleaning, Chibi must work to heal the family and make them happy again. There is also a mystery in the house, namely some of the toys in the house come alive at night. Chibi must also find out why this is so.

How does syntax work? What are the basic units and how are they combined?

As in all good games, the syntax of *Chibi-Robo* fits very well with its game mechanics, that is, with the actions players need to take to play the game. Since Chibi is only four inches tall and must get all over the house (e.g., upstairs, to the tops of chests of drawers, to chandeliers, and so forth), the game focuses on objects and their parts as these are relevant to climbing and otherwise accessing things when you are four inches tall. One interesting part of the game is that the characters speak in gibberish and so the player needs to read their emotions in terms of the context of communication. Just as Chibi has to access the physical environment in ways available to a four-inch creature, he must also access the emotional environment of the family, pets, and animate toys in ways available to a creature who cannot talk.

The syntax of *Chibi-Robo* is quite interesting. It uses the parts-and-wholes syntax of everyday objects that we are all familiar with (e.g., chests of drawers are composed of feet, drawers, flat tops, and maybe a mirror)—though it presents these in "blocky" images—but focuses on them from the perspective of a four-inch creature. This means that the game world of *Chibi-Robo* has the syntax we associate with spaces and objects in houses, but attaches a distinctive semantics to that syntax (see below).

As in many games, another aspect of *Chibi-Robo*'s syntax is various sorts of meters that show up on the screen. Note that this game keeps the meter for elapsed time (top left of screen) and the meter for time left on Chibi's batteries (bottom right) separate. How such meters and other HUD (Heads-Up Display) devices are combined or not is part of a game's syntax. In this case, separating the two meters creates a challenge in the game, since the player must not let time run out before all Chibi's battery power is gone (otherwise Chibi will "die"). The player must look back and forth between the two meters as the player scans the environment for ways to get to places and do things in time.

How does semantics work?

What universe of discourse is involved?

The universe of discourse for *Chibi-Robo* is composed of a four-inch battery-powered house-cleaning robot, with various skills and tools, and of people and objects we are all familiar with in the real world. Chibi also has a little house of his own and an advisor and pal named Telly Vision (who speaks for Chibi). Chibi eventually discovers a much larger, but inoperative, robot in the basement (Giga-Robo). Finally, Chibi eventually makes contacts with aliens and a time-machine.

How was the universe of discourse determined?

The universe of discourse is partly traditional with some Japanese games which simulate aspects of real life (e.g., growing plants or cooking) in a fantasy sort of way. The presence of a small and large robot in the house, toys that are animate at night, spider-like robots (called Spydorz), aliens, and a time-machine all add to the universe a sense of fiction, science fiction, and futurism. As I said above, some characteristically Japanese themes help shape the universe of discourse.

How are meanings assigned from the universe of discourse?

Objects and their parts are assigned meanings in terms of Chibi-Robo's functions and tasks. Things like paw prints across the floor (as in Figure 9.1) mean "things to clean". Drawers that are open in the right way mean "stairs to climb". Small gaps mean "something to fly over with Chibi's built in helicopter blades". In general everything in the environment has to be assigned a meaning in terms of cleaning and access or in terms of possibilities to make the family happy or find out why some of the toys are alive. Chibi is simultaneously a cleaner and detective.

What is the avatar?

How does the avatar function as an identity?

Chibi is designed to want to make everyone happy. Despite being a robot, Chibi is an emotional force seeking to do good. He helps the family, he helps the animate toys, and eventually he helps Giga-Robo. Japanese games and manga (comic books) often focus on what makes something human. In these games and manga, things that do not look human are often more human in behavior and emotions than things that do look human. Such games and manga also often play with images of and themes about "animate dolls". Of course, Chibi is a type of animate doll.

How does the avatar function as a surrogate body?

Chibi is four-inches tall. He has batteries that need to be recharged, though as he "levels up" by getting "Happy Points" his batteries improve and he can stay out longer. The fact that Chibi is four inches tall is crucial to the game's mechanics and to the story in the game as well. One thing that I very much enjoyed about the game was being able to experience the world from the perspective of such a small good-hearted creature.

How does the avatar function as a tool-kit?

In the game, the player can purchase items and power ups with Moolah (money), as well as use scrap metal to build robotic helpers that ease Chibi's navigation of the house. Chibi has a "Chibi-Copter" that he can use to reach far-off points or to safely fly down from high places. He has a blaster that eliminates obstacles and fends off the Spydorz. He also has a radar to detect hidden objects; a toothbrush to clean up stains; a coffee mug to hide in; a spoon he can use to dig holes; and a squirter to hold fluids and squirt them. Chibi-Robo can also gain special costumes throughout the game, each of which has its own unique function (e.g., he can put on a dog suit so he can communicate with the dog in the house). At certain ranks, a company named "Citrusoft" will send the player bonus batteries, allowing Chibi-Robo to roam longer before having to recharge. Finally, Chibi is a skilled climber.

How are affordances and effective abilities aligned?

Players must look for affordances to clean and otherwise make the family happy that match Chibi's skills and tools. The fact that he is four inches tall makes this alignment challenging and interesting. We humans are used to aligning with the world as mid-sized creatures. In this game, we get to see and feel what it is like to align to a world when you are very small.

How does X-ray vision function?

What are the relevant details for aligning affordances and effective abilities?

In the game world all sorts of aspects of the world are relevant that are not relevant usually to us big creatures in the real world. If a drawer is cracked open, this can make it a step. Since Chibi must recharge his batteries, players have to pay avid attention to time and distance from an electric outlet.

What tools are being used to supplement "seeing" and interaction?

Chibi has a radar and he has tools that allow him to see the world in terms of what needs cleaning and how to clean it. He has meters that make the player focus on time and distance. Players must choose challenges that can be done in the time Chibi's batteries will allow at that point in the game.

How is meaning being situated? How are situated meanings created?

What is the context? How is it being construed and constructed?

The context is a house seen as things to clean and people, toys, and another robot to help. The context is construed from the point of view of a four-inch robot with limited skills and no ability to talk for himself.

What are the relevant aspects of the context and how is relevance being determined?

The relevant aspects of context are the parts of the environment that allow access to a four-inch creature. Also relevant is anything that helps indicate why Giga-Robo is not operating and why some toys are alive, as well as anything that speaks as to why the family is unhappy and what will make them happy is also relevant. *How is relevance being determined?* Relevance is determined by the size and skills of Chibi and the limits of his batteries. It is determined as well by whatever will earn Chibi "Happy Points". Unlike some games, players in *Chibi-Robo* cannot choose to be "bad" and not help. If they do the game goes nowhere.

How is "packaging"—how units are combined (syntax)—helping to create situated meaning? What were alternatives ways things could have been packaged? What does it mean that these alternatives were not used?

Chibi starts the game composed of a robot body and an electrical cord and plug. The tools he can use (e.g., his Chibi-Copter) are bought in the game's store (for fictional money) or found in the environment as Chibi and the player level up by earning "Happy Points". This means that the player earns and composes Chibi's parts. Chibi becomes more skilled as the player gains more skill. Had Chibi been "fully formed" at the beginning, the game would have been a very different game.

How does the sequence and flow of sentences, utterances, or activities work to help create situated meanings?

This is one of the most interesting aspects of the game. I will discuss it below, when we finish this brief summary. Suffice it to say here, that in *Chibi-Robo* the player's sequence of choices and actions construct the game's levels. What this means is that the "player's story"—the player's personal trajectory of choices and actions—is quite strong and meaningful in the game.

What is the role of story (top-down, authored stories or stories produced in the course of interaction); cultural, social, scientific, or other sorts of theories, models, schemas, or frames; and beliefs, values, and ideologies?

Chibi-Robo, as we have said, deals with a number of Japanese cultural themes and values, especially as these appear in Japanese anime. The game has a top-down story that makes clear, bit by bit, what is going on in Chibi's world. The story makes what the player is doing lucid and meaningful. I will not disclose the story (it would be a "spoiler" for anyone who wants to play the game), but I will say the ending of *Chibi-Robo* made me cry.

How is a "player's story" being constructed by the choices, decisions, actions, interactions, successes and failures the "player" experiences as he or she talks, acts, and plays? (Here I use "player" for anyone speaking, writing, acting on the world, or playing a game.)

The player's story in *Chibi-Robo* is composed of a set of choices and actions that compose an emotional arch to the game, an arch that fits wonderfully with the top-down story, imbuing it with meaning and emotion it might not otherwise have had. As in many games, players can invest their energy and attention to different aspects of the game. For me, working to bring Giga-Robo alive again, to find out why he was "dead", and what he had to do with the toys being animate was a fun part of the game, a part that was amply rewarded by the end of the game's top-down story.

As I promised above, I will now discuss the question *"How does the sequence and flow of sentences, utterances, or activities work to help create situated meanings"* in more detail. This is a place where *Chibi-Robo* shines. *Chibi-Robo* is an "open world" game in the sense that the player can go anywhere he or she pleases within the constraints of Chibi's batteries. Unlike some games, *Chibi-Robo* does not direct the player's path in any very overt way.

When Chibi-Robo comes out of his (or her?) little home for the first time, the player is confronted with a large world (for a small robot) but with very limited battery time. What this means is that the players must find a problem to solve that is close to home and close to the nearest electric plug. In turn, this means players must learn to scan only the part of the world nearest them to find affordances for solving problems and gaining their first "Happy Points". The game is training the player's vision in a constrained space.

Essentially in *Chibi-Robo* battery time determines the game's levels. Unlike games with overt level design, the player is never aware of levels changing. However, the amount of time on Chibi's batteries determines the relevant physical space within which problems can be solved and the problems that exist at that "level". The problems closer to home—the ones the player will face first—are the easiest and constitute a sort of hidden tutorial. As Chibi and the player gain more skills, the player can wander further afield and make more open choices.

This design feature means that players are guided (without really feeling it) pretty strongly in terms of the initial sequences of their actions and, then, when they learn how to play the game, they are free to create and revel in their own sequences of choices, strategies, and actions as they make their own player's story.

In a sense, in *Chibi-Robo* the player is initially guided and then left free to create the discourse of the game in the sense of the sequence of meaningful turns (probes and responses from the world) or actions. Discourse is partly about the flow of time and *Chibi-Robo* makes the flow of time an important ingredient (actually a game mechanic) of play.

Chibi-Robo's design solves one of the main problems of productive problem-based learning (and most video games are forms of problem-based learning). The problem is this: learners feel empowered if they are left free to choose the problems they want to solve, but if they choose problems that are too hard at the beginning they often hit on creative solutions that do not, however, lead to generative patterns for solving future and even easier problems (Gee 2004, 2007). They can go down a "garden path". Learners need initially to see problems that lend themselves to teaching core skills in the problem space and that lead to generative solutions that will be aspects of solving future harder problems.

Chibi-Robo brilliantly constrains you in a meaningful and motivating way at the beginning—a way that makes sense in story terms and in terms of *Chibi-Robo*'s game mechanics. The player co-creates an initial tutorial and later level design while all the while feeling freely at play. Of course, learning to do this sort of "design" for ourselves (or seeking mentorship) in the real world when we confront a new problem space (a new set of problems in a given domain) is a crucial skill, though one rarely taught in school.

Chibi-Robo is a conversation between a player as Chibi and a world seen through the eyes, body, tools, and values of a four-inch house-cleaning happiness-producing robot. The world looks much like the one we live in in our own homes, but it looks entirely different as we interrogate that world with a new body, tools, and identity.

A core part of living a productive human life is learning to see the world in new ways as we gain new identities, skills, values, and tools. In the act we gain new ideas about affordances for action in the world, actions that we hope will make us and our world better. Games like *Chibi-Robo* let us play with this very basic and important human capacity. Good games give us new tools for seeing the real world in new ways and for seeing new possibilities for action (the *Portal* games are another great example).

It is interesting to compare how control works in our earlier example from school and in this example from *Chibi-Robo*. *Chibi-Robo* controls and regulates the player at the beginning of the game in a way that makes sense (since Chibi only has a short battery life to begin with), is part of the game play, and is inherently connected to what players will need to do and learn later when they gain enough basic skills to go off on their own, without the game designer holding their hand.

In the school example, where the little girl is told "not to go ahead" and to "just clam down", these commands are not integrally tied to what is to be learned and mastered (reading) and the control the girl is experiencing here is not part of the "game" of reading, but of a "game" of regulation that has become detached from content learning like learning to read. Control here may make much less sense to the girl than it does to players in *Chibi-Robo*.

It is ironic, perhaps, that Chibi, too, cannot "go ahead" at the beginning of the game. But he (and the player) knows why (his battery life is too short) and sees it is an integral part of game play (learning to monitor time out and battery life and relate them to choices of how far to go to solve problems) where this control will lead to much greater freedom later. And, of course, in Chibi's world being happy is not a problem to be controlled, but a goal to achieve for oneself and others.

10

METAL GEAR SOLID

Metal Gear Solid 4

In this chapter, I analyze *Metal Gear Solid 4: Guns of the Patriots* (hereafter "*MGS4*"). I use some of the tools developed earlier. I will argue that in some respects *MGS4* is a virtual tutorial on what it means to play video games and what sort of conversations they can set up (Gee 2009).

It will be clear from this analysis that a discourse analysis analyzes language/ worlds/games "in use", that is, as we humans use them in real contexts. We study how aspects of a game's design afford a certain sort of interactive conversation given a specific player's desires, values, and skills.

Story in *MGS4*

Seth Schiesel, lead video game writer for the *New York Times*, had this to say about *Metal Gear Solid 4: Guns of the Patriots*:

> I play games because of the freedom they afford. In contrast to a book or a film or a theater performance, a game lets me decide what happens next, or at least lets me operate under the illusion that my actions matter. ... Metal Gear Solid 4 is not like that. Instead it is a linear narrative by the Japanese designer Hideo Kojima. You, the player, are along for the ride. M.G.S. 4 is Mr. Kojima's world, and you are just passing through for the moment while he tells you where to go next, what to do and more or less how to do it.

Seth is a lot younger than I am and he does, indeed, know his game stuff. But, as I argued earlier, game play is a matter of a conversation between a player and a game world. Seth is reviewing not the game, but the conversation he had with it. I had a different conversation with the game. Mine was great. Seth's not so great.

Despite all the efforts of Games Studies people to search for a grand unified category of games, there is none. Different types of video games are different. Different types of players are different. And the two interact in all sorts of different ways. There are no grand theories to be had.

My conversation with *MGS4* isn't yours and yours isn't mine. And mine isn't Seth's. And that is the freedom I love in video games. That said, of course basic design features of a game shape the conversation. And, indeed, Seth is discussing one of these design features, namely the way in which *MGS4* has a linear narrative that makes for more linear sorts of play than Seth likes.

When I say my *MGS4* isn't yours and yours isn't mine, I don't mean the obvious truth—a truth about any media: different people have different interpretations. That ho-hum truth is true of books, films, games and any and every use of language.

What I mean is that in my *MGS4* game play I (Jim Gee) am Solid Snake, not you, not Seth, not even the game's designer, Mr. Kojima.

At the end of his review, Seth says:

> Of course, by the time those credits did roll, I was ready for the M.G.S. 4 experience to be over. Not that I hadn't enjoyed it. It was probably the best near-future action movie I had ever seen. But I was ready to make some of my own choices. In short, I was ready to play a game.

MGS4 indeed has very long, gorgeous, exciting, over-the-top by any standards cut scenes. The final one lasts well over an hour. *MGS4* is, indeed, a great action movie.

However, when I played the game the second time around, on a harder mode, I cut off all the cut scenes and just played the game. There are players who even cut off all the cut scenes the first time around.

I would argue that cutting off the cut scenes at least the second time around is what Mr. Kojima wants you to do. It is what the game is designed to have you do. In my view as a gamer, *MGS4* is one of those games that if you have played it only once, you haven't really played "the game". It's because to play *MGS4* "well", you have to be a good Snake and you are a better Snake the second or third time around. That is, at least, the nature of the conversation I had with the game.

Seth's review brings up two vexed questions for gamers: What is the role of the top-down story in a game? What is the role of cut scenes? These questions are connected in that very often a game's top-down story is carried in part by cut scenes.

Some players love the stories in games. I don't. I can rarely follow them. For me, the game's story sets the scene, conveys emotions, and makes clear what things in the world and my actions in the game mean. I rarely put the whole story together, the way I would do with a film or a book. I care more about the player's story (my story). This I seem to share with Seth.

The story in a game, as we have said, helps determine the game's "universe of discourse". It tells us what is in the world, why it is there, what things mean, and the ways in which we can and cannot act in the world. We will see that the story in *MGS4* plays this role in a striking way. It makes clear that Snake is different this time (in this the last game in the series in which Solid Snake will appear) and it makes clear that players need to think about how to be a "good Snake" under arduous conditions.

Let me start with one example of what I mean by thinking about being a "good Snake". In *MSG4*, unlike any game I can remember, playing well can sometimes mean playing badly. Most anyone would think—especially if they are thinking of sports, say—that to play well is to get things right and do well. But this is not always so in *MGS4*.

In *MGS4* Snake is sick, old, and tired (due to intentional gene manipulation of Big Boss's clones, of which Snake is one). He regularly grunts and holds his back in pain. He has to inject himself with a special medicine even to keep going at all.

There is a moment in *MGS4* where Snake has to remember a code. Surely forgetting the code is not getting things right and doing well. But when Snake (my Snake, me) forgets the code—hey, I'm 65 years old—it becomes part of the story. Otacon is already worried about Snake's physical and mental deterioration—as is Snake—and this just confirms, as he acknowledges, for him and Snake both, that things are getting worse, as indeed they are.

When I was playing the game second time round, Snake (I) got the code right and Otacon was relieved. Which way is right? Which way is "well played"? Who is the better Snake? My Snake the first time around is not even my Snake the second time around. I fashion him anew each time.

So when I play badly—not remembering a code, messing up on sneaking, or miss getting a perfect head shot—when I have to make do and recover after my mess up—am I playing well? Am I playing Snake as the sick and tired old man he is in *MGS4*? Or am I playing well when I and Snake rise above all the pain and succeed in fine fashion—as a hero like Snake would do—save for the fact that even in some of the cut scenes in *MGS4* he doesn't do it here? Which way is being a good Snake for this game?

You see *that* is what it is all about for me: being a good Snake in this specific game. And this is a game that ends when Snake's father (Big Boss) tells him that the world no longer needs any Snakes, therefore: "Go be a man". What does it mean to be a good Snake? What does it mean to "be a man"? What is the difference?

These questions are set up by the game's story and the way it sets up the game's universe of discourse. In this case, the world contains a transformed Snake, an old and dying one. This sets up, for me, an interpretive framework that makes the story and game play interact as I think about playing the game well, but as both an old deteriorating Snake and old deteriorating man. I can intersect my own real-world identity as an old man with Snake's identity as an aging hero crawling to his last stand.

I have been struck by how little much of the commentary about *MGS4* on the Internet (most of it written by people a good deal younger than me) makes of Snake's age and condition in the game. But, for me, this was the first video game I had played where the hero was my age. Solid Snake has always been one of my heroes in video games. He was before always the young, strong, virile superhero. Now he is more mortal, more a "man" (human).

Snake's condition—that this is his last act as Solid Snake—makes us reinterpret lots of the *Metal Gear Solid* game world. Things and acts in it take on new nuances and emotional meanings now that Snake is a wounded warrior faced with his own limitations for the first time.

X-ray vision

As we argued, video games are not really (just) pretty pictures ("eye candy"), but "signs" to be "read". We must look through the rich details of a game's graphics to see just those details or aspects of the world that are relevant to action, goals, and problem solving. Another way to put this is that gamers see the relevant details and aspects of the game world as "signs" with meaning, just like words in a language.

To play well you must read the signs well. In *MGS4* reading the signs well means being a good Snake. What does that mean? Well, let's take a quick tour through *MGS4*—because *MGS4* makes a big deal (indeed) out of reading signs.

MGS4 regularly plays with the medium to get the player to reflect on the fact that he or she is playing a video game. Let me just say that *MGS4* constantly "goes meta" in the sense that it makes you *think about* the fact that you are playing a video game (the meta level) and does not let you just play it and forget about it.

Remember those great film-like cut scenes? In some of them we see rain or ice on the camera lens. This makes us well aware that the action is being filmed. But wait, it can't be being filmed, there is no camera, this is a video game.

It's a regular film technique to do stuff like this (showing muck on the camera lens) to make the viewer aware the action is being filmed and filmed from a certain perspective. It calls direct attention to the medium (film) as a medium, rather than seeing the medium as a transparent window onto the world.

But Mr. Kojima is calling attention to the wrong medium: this is a video game and not a film and there is no camera. He is, perhaps, calling wry attention to all the controversy about how games should not be movies (a la Seth) while they get more movie-like all the time. And, of course, he is signaling, as well, what genre of Hollywood film he wants you to compare his cut scenes to, i.e., avant garde action films.

But no matter why he is doing it, Mr. Kojima is surely telling us to pay attention to the signs—to the rain and ice on the camera. He wants these signs to signal the fact that this is all artificial, not real, not even a transparent window onto the world, even a fantasy world. It's a video game pretending to be a movie, knowing all the while it's a video game.

MGS4 constantly makes references to earlier *MGS* games as games. It constantly makes reference, as well, to the fact that you are playing a video, even a violent one, and even suggests that maybe such games are training you for real violence and, hey, maybe you shouldn't be doing this. This is a wry comment on the controversies over video game violence. *MGS4* even makes several references to the fact that you are playing on a Play Station 3. The signs that you are playing a game are rubbed in your face.

Some specific examples that I love—and there are many in the game: Snake ends up in exactly the place where in an earlier game he fought and defeated a tank by throwing grenades into it. I remember. I did it. Did it well, if I say so myself. But Otacon tells Snake that he has checked with an expert and the expert tells him that no individual could defeat a tank that way. It's impossible. He asks Snake how he did it; he marvels that he did it—how did he do it? Maybe it was just a game, not real. Snake just grunts.

Another example: Deep into the game, Otacon tells Snake that the disk needs to be switched. Asks him if he sees a second disk. Snake says no. Otacon says something like, oh, I remember, this is Play Station 3 with a blue ray disk technology. We don't need to switch disks any more like in the old days. He then marvels at the wonders of new technologies and Snake tells him to "get a grip".

Here is another example: One level starts off with the exact 2D game level from an earlier game. This is a level I remember very well indeed. I have even used screen shots from it in my talks. You (re-)play the old game a bit and then all of a sudden, it stops and you see that Snake was having a dream. Hey, he dreams video game dreams.

Yet another example: During those gorgeous cut scenes a little "x" comes on in the corner of the screen every once in a while. If you keep pushing "x" on the controller you see flashes of scenes from earlier games—scenes thematically connected to what you are seeing in the cut scene. The cut scene is totally realistic looking, but the flash back is out of an earlier game and, thus, looks much more "primitive".

This juxtaposition of realism and less realistic graphics from earlier games surely tells the player that no matter how realistic *MGS4* looks—thanks to that wonderful Play Station 3 technology—it is still a video game and, in core respects, not different than the earlier games, games which were worse as "eye candy", but good as games. But then it can't be the graphics that make a game and the superb graphics of *MGS4* aren't what makes it a great game.

Indeed, *MGS4* is one of the most realistic looking video games in history. But it regularly undercuts that realism to underscore that you are playing a video game—and not just a video game, but an *MGS* game. Not only do we get all the references to the earlier games. We also get decidedly unrealistic conventions (carried over from the earlier games) like a question mark or an exclamation point showing up over an enemy's head when he thinks he has discovered Snake (the question mark) or when he definitely has discovered Snake (the exclamation point). If question marks and exclamation marks are not signs to be read, I don't know what are.

So throughout Mr. Kojima makes it clear that gamers have to "read" signs: signs like the water on the camera, the question and exclamation marks, the flash backs to earlier games, the wry comments on the fact that you are playing a game and that what Snake has done earlier (and, therefore, probably now, too) can't be real. Why this obsession with signs and reading signs?

Two reasons: First, reading signs of a certain sort in a certain way is what you have to do when playing any video game. This is what we earlier called "X-ray vision".

Second: This—reading signs in a certain way—is *especially* what you have to do in *MGS* games in a *special* way, not just because they are stealth games, but because that is one of the things Snake is good at (reading signs) and you are supposed to be a good Snake.

We have come to the heart of the matter. Snake is the ultimate video game character because he lives, breathes, and acts in the virtual world of *MSG* games just the way good video game players are supposed to play any video game. And what does *that* mean?

It means that Snake looks for affordances, just like savvy gamers do. In a deep sense Snake is playing a video game. So this does sound weird, so let me hasten to tell you what I mean.

Ok, imagine you are playing a video game (actually playing, not watching a cut scene). What do you do? Well, you could just rush off and button mash, but that is, in most good games a good way to a bad result. No, you pay close attention to your environment so that you can discover how and where aspects of that environment can serve as affordances for you to accomplish goals, given the effective abilities Snake (and remember his abilities are attenuated in this game) has and you have.

In *MGS4*, the goals you accomplish are: (a) Snake's goals (the ones the game tells you he has); (b) goals you have set for yourself as a player (e.g., to finish in under nine hours); and (c) what I call Snake/Jim goals. Snake/Jim goals are ones that Snake can have (they are allowed but not determined by the game design) and that you have chosen to have for the way you want to play Snake (e.g., killing no one).

As we have seen, an affordance is something in the environment that you can use to accomplish a goal, but it is only an affordance if you have the skill to use it. So to pay attention to affordances means to pay attention to how your skills match up with aspects of the environment to take advantage of them as affordances for your goals. Using *MGS4* as an example, you have to pay attention to the skills Snake has. These are the skills the game designers have given him (e.g., using his camouflage outfit to meld into the environment). Snake's skills actually change on different difficulty levels and even change in different contexts of the game (e.g., when he is overstressed in *MGS4*).

You also have to pay attention to your own skills as a player. For example, say you are just no good with the timing of the grab command and, thus, no good at grabbing enemies from behind (this sucks for you because you must do this in one of the boss battles in the game). For you, enemies with their back to you are not an affordance for grabbing and you will engage them in some other way (shoot them, sneak past them, get the Mark 3 to distract them).

Finally, you have to pay attention to the skills you choose to use in being your own kind of Snake. Even if you are good at sniper rifles—and so far away enemies are affordances for sniping—you might still choose to sneak by all enemies, giving up sniping as an option. You choose not to let far away enemies be affordances for your sniper skills, because you want to be a sneaky Snake.

So playing video games as a savvy gamer is matching skills to aspects of the environment that can become affordances to carry out goals. In *MGS4* this means carefully observing the environment to find good hiding places, vantage points for stealth attacks or sniper shots, paths around enemies, or weak spots in a boss's attack, and much more, all with due regard for your own skills as a player and what sort of Snake you want to be and can be (given those skills).

Mr. Kojima, the game's lead designer, is well aware of all this, even if he would not use my language. In *MGS4* he gives Snake a device that just shouts out my affordance theory: it's all about matching your skills with your environment.

Snake has a special suit that allows him to meld into his environment so well he becomes camouflaged and virtually invisible. With the suit, every part of the environment is an affordance for Snake to disappear. Without the suit he cannot do it and no part of the environment offers him any such affordance.

Now, you may think my analysis here is too fanciful. However, Mr. Kojima devotes one level of *MGS4* to a tutorial on the matter. In this level, Snake has to use his "Solid Eye", a device that gives him hyper vision where he can see foot prints, enemies, and other "signs" (like where loot such as ammo and rations are on the ground) clearly, even in bad light conditions. Raiden tells Snake that he must track the people who took Naomi, all the while watching out carefully for enemy soldiers.

Snake says he really has no tracking skills (oops, that's a problem). Therefore, nothing in the environment is going to be an affordance for Snake to track.

Raiden comes to the rescue. He gives Snake a tutorial on how expert trackers—like Native Americans—use all their senses to pay attention to every little sign (e.g., broken twigs, heavier or lighter foot prints, the distribution of the weight shown by a foot print, sounds, disturbances however small in the environment). He tells Snake he must read the signs carefully (see, it's all about reading signs). After the tutorial, Otacon coaches Snake through the whole thing.

So Snake (and you) learn to pay very close attention to the environment (with the aid of the Solid Eye tool) to read all the signs, no matter how subtle, to use them as affordances to know where to go—which path out of many choices to follow—so you can pursue Naomi's kidnappers without being seen. Snake is getting a lesson and so are you the player, a lesson on tracking and, I argue, a lesson on playing video games, at least games like *MGS4*. Because, after all, Snake is usually good (though not this time) at reading the signs to use his environment to his advantage—it's his "super power"—and you need to be, too, if you are going to be a good gamer and a good Snake.

I must say that my Snake was not all that good at tracking. And remember he said he wasn't. And he is just learning. And he is old (so am I) and sick and tired. So this is another case where not doing well is doing well (being Snake as he is). But he gets through (not all that badly, for Snake or for me or for my Snake, I must say—especially the second time round and remember I said above that the second time round is important, though I haven't gotten to that yet).

So that's what good gamers do: match skills to the environment to create affordances for accomplishing goals. So Snake and I both got a lesson from Raiden,

Otacon, and Mr. Kojima on the whole theory. But above I said Snake was special because his whole being as Snake—what he does, what he is—is acting in just this way, as a good gamer. It is like he is playing a game and that's why Otacon keeps telling him—and you—that he is (and you are) playing a video game.

Being human

To be a good gamer is to be a good Snake; to be a good Snake is to be a good gamer. But remember, Snake's father told us that after our heroic accomplishments in *MGS4*, the world needs no more Snakes—"go be a man". Perhaps, Mr. Kojima wants us to stop gaming and go out and change the world.

No, that's not what he means, I think. Or, at least, not all that he means. In "Self, video games, and pedagogy" Jenny Wright (2008) compares heroes in Native American myths and heroes in role-playing video games. She says: "[t]he sense of achievement you gain from becoming an expert manipulator of any environment is addictive and affirming".

Being a good gamer and being a good Snake in fact requires the core skill, not just of heroes, but of "a man" or "a woman"—of an effective, efficacious human being—and that skill is: becoming adept at gaining and matching skills with different aspects of the environment to use them as affordances to accomplish important goals.

To play *MGS4* well means to be a good Snake. And that means to be a good gamer. And that means to be a hero. And that means to be a thoughtful human. Pay attention to those affordances.

Every hero, every human, has different skills, different desires. Every hero, every human, matches skills and desires to environments to accomplish goals differently. Every player plays Snake differently. My Snake is not yours, yours is not mine. My life is not yours, yours is not mine. My excellence is not yours, yours is not mine. As long as we are trying to play well, to honor Snake, to be good Snakes, the best we can, we are all the hero crawling to the last boss to become "a man", "a woman", "a human".

But why does Seth have to play *MGS4* a second time and maybe a third too? Because each time around, you're a better Snake.

And why are all those gorgeous cut scenes there? Just to tell you that Snake is a hero and what sort of hero he is. Snake *is* a hero and *you* can't let him down.

But, remember, too, the best Snake (in fact the one you have to be on the hardest level of the game) is a sneaky non-lethal Snake, the Snake that always leaves the Hollywood action movie in favor of disappearing unseen, unheard into his environment, all the while accomplishing his goals. (On "The Boss Extreme Difficulty" level, you must complete the game in under five hours with no alerts, no humans killed, and no continues, while using no health replenishing items and foregoing the Octocamo stealth suit.)

Being a sneaky Snake is hard this time around, in *MGS4*, the final game. Snake is old. So am I. So it's ok to make mistakes. But we play again. Make fewer mistakes. Snake and I get better—perhaps, too, just a bit younger.

And why is it ok to cut off those cut scenes? Because I know Snake already and have long wanted to be him and have been him now four times. I see he is old now. But he is still my hero.

Here is my personal reflection, after playing the game, on the fight with the boss "Crying Wolf":

> I have tracked her unique prints in the snow (and they said I was no good at tracking!). But I am far away. She does not see me or hear me. She does not know I am here. But I know she is there. I wait. The world is covered in wind and snow and ice and mist. It is a pure white out. There is no visibility. Then all of a sudden the mists part. I have waited patiently. I am ready. My silenced sniper bullet hurls through the air for a perfect head shot. Unseen. Unheard. Crying Wolf is defeated. I have been a good Snake. Even though I am old. Oh, but I will be a better Snake next time around. I'll use non-lethal ammo. I'll just stun her and quietly move on.

Avatars

This analysis makes clear what sort of avatar Solid Snake is in this game for me. His body is old and weak, its physical skills attenuated. His identity is as an aging hero making a last stand before he becomes just a man. The tool-kit he gives the player contains his Strong Eye, his camouflage suit, his radar, and several other devices, most of which have to do with reading the environment.

We have argued that people in the real world confront and interact with each other and with the world not directly, but in terms of a social identity we have also referred to as an avatar. When we are acting out an avatar, in a game or in real life, we are being a "kind of person".

The "kind of person" Solid Snake is in *MGS4* is defined by the game's story, cut scenes, the earlier games, and my own play in those game and in *MGS4*. An avatar is an odd thing in many ways. Solid Snake is not me, but I play him and when I do, he and I meld in a certain way. It is not his goals or mine alone that determine how "we" play, but the both of us together determine how we play. The game allows "us" (Snake and I) to create what I have called the "player's story", my own unique history as Snake/Jim. In the next chapter I will argue that avatars (social identities) in the real world behave in the same way. All avatars involve what I will call in the next chapter a "projective identity".

11

PROJECTIVE IDENTITY

Projective identity

In this chapter I want take up the idea of an avatar in more depth. I am using this word for avatars in games and social identities in the world. Here I will argue that these two things—avatars in games and social identities in the world—are more similar than many might think. Both crucially involve what I will call here a "projective identity", an idea that this chapter will be devoted to.

We can get at the notion of projective identity by asking two related questions: What is the deep pleasure human beings get from video games? What is the relationship between video games and real life? I believe that good video games are extensions of life in a quite strict sense, since they recruit and externalize some of the most fundamental features of how human beings orient in and to the real world (e.g., aligning affordances and effective abilities), especially when they are operating at their best.

In this chapter, I will argue that good video games create a "projective identity". They create a double-sided stance towards the world (virtual or real) in terms of which we humans see the world simultaneously as a project imposed on us and as a site onto which we can actively project our desires, values, and goals (Gee 2007). A projective identity is a melded identity, a melding of self and avatar in a way that gives rise to a new sort of being.

Consider two related claims about playing video games:

1 In a video game, players often inhabit (accept, take on) the goals of a virtual character in a virtual world. The virtual world is designed to be attuned to or allow for the accomplishment of these goals.
2 In a video game, a virtual character also instantiates the goals of a real-world player. The virtual world is designed to invite the real-world player to form certain sorts of goals of his or her own and not others.

The real interest is in the interaction between these claims. But let's get clear on what each one means first. We can start with the first claim: In video games, players inhabit the goals of a virtual character in a virtual world. The virtual world is designed to be attuned to those goals. In a video game the real-world player gains a surrogate; that is, the virtual character the player is playing, his or her avatar. By "inhabit" I mean that you, the player, act in the game as if the goals of your surrogate are your goals.

Virtual characters have virtual minds and virtual bodies. They become the player's surrogate mind and body. You may wonder what I mean by the "mind" of a virtual character. What I mean is this: as a player, you must—on the basis of what you learn about the game's story and the game's virtual world—attribute certain mental states (beliefs, values, goals, feelings, attitudes, and so forth) to the virtual character. You must take these to be the character's mental states; you must take them as a basis for explaining the character's actions in the world.

By "attuned" I mean that the virtual character, that character's goals, and the virtual world of the game are designed to mesh or fit together in certain ways. The virtual character (in terms of the character's skills and attributes) and the virtual world are built to go together such that the character's goals are easier to reach in certain ways than they are in others, based on the nature of the character (the avatar as an identity, body, and tool-kit) and the world.

Let's consider an example. Take the game *Thief: Deadly Shadows*. In this game the player plays the master thief, Garrett. In inhabiting Garrett's body (whether playing the game in first-person or third-person mode), the player inherits specific powers and limitations. In inhabiting Garrett's body, with its powers and limitations, the player also inhabits Garrett's specific goals; goals having to do with stealing, infiltrating, and stealthily removing or sneaking past guards to accomplish specific story-related ends in the game. Given Garrett's powers and limitations, these goals are easier to reach in some ways than others within the specific virtual world of this game.

The virtual world in *Thief*—the world through which you as Garrett move—is a world designed to interact with Garrett's powers and limitations in terms of specific affordances and disaffordances. These affordances and disaffordances do not reside in the world alone, but in the combination of the specific mind/body Garrett brings to that world and the way in which that world encourages or discourages that specific mind/body in terms of possible actions.

It is a world of shadows and hiding places, a world well fit for Garrett's superb (mental and physical) skills at hiding, waiting, watching, and sneaking. It affords hiding and sneaking of all sorts. It is not a world well made for outright confrontations and frontal fights: in this world, Garrett can find no guns or weapons much beyond a small dagger, and the spaces that would allow outright fights with multiple guards are pretty cramped, allowing guards easily to surround Garrett.

And, indeed, this is all to the good—the world fits well with the mind/body Garrett brings to the game—since Garrett most certainly has grave limitations when it comes to fighting outright in the light. He can shoot an arrow unseen from the shadows or he can sneak past guards, but he's quite weak when he shows himself in the light for open battle. The way the world is made, the way that Garrett's mind/body is made, and how they mesh, has major consequences for the sorts of effective plans and goals (you as) Garrett can make and carry out.

So, in video games the world is made to fit with the character (avatar) and the character (avatar) is made to fit with the world. The world of *Thief* fits Garrett and Garrett fits that world. Mario would be lost in the *Thief* world and Garrett would be lost in any of the worlds in the *Mario* games.

Video game creates a three-way interaction among the virtual character's mind/body, the character's goals, and the design features of the virtual world in terms of affordances for effective action. They all fit together:

> virtual character $\leftrightarrow$ goals $\leftrightarrow$ virtual world.

The player, of course, must find the right fit or match between these three things. In a game, the virtual character's powers and limitations mesh with the way in which the game's virtual world is designed in quite specific ways so that the virtual character's goals can be accomplished better in some ways than others. Finding this mesh or fit—"sweet spots" for effective action—is, of course, one of the key skills required in playing a video game. You *can* play *Thief* as an out and out fighting game, eschewing stealth, but you will be fighting the mesh (that discourages such actions) between Garrett's mind/body (your surrogate mind/body), his goals, and the virtual world of the game all the way.

So, now, onto the second claim: In video games a virtual character instantiates the goals of a real-world player. The virtual world of the game is designed to invite the real-world player to form certain sorts of goals of his or her own and not others. According to the first claim, in a game like *Thief: Deadly Shadows*, you, the player, see the world from Garrett's perspective and need to find ways to use the mesh ("fit") in the world among Garrett's mind/body, his goals, and the design of the virtual world to carry out his goals effectively.

But things work the other way round, as well. Garrett becomes a reservoir that can be filled with the player's own desires, intentions, and goals. By placing your own goals within Garrett—by seeing them as Garrett's goals—you can enact your desires in Garrett's virtual world. But note that this is a process that works well only if you carefully consider the mesh ("fit") that exists in the game among Garrett's mind/body, his goals, and the design of the virtual world. This is the only way in which your own goals will be effectively added to Garrett's and accomplished, since the game will resist goals that fall outside this mesh. In this sense, your own personal goals must become Garrett-like goals, goals that flow from his (virtual) mind and body as they are placed in this specific game world.

Let me give an example. At one point in *Thief*, Garrett needs to break into a museum to get an important object. This is Garrett's goal and you need to inhabit him and see the game world from the perspective of his affordances in this particular virtual world if you are to play this part of the game successfully. This is just claim 1.

But let's say that you as a player decide that you want to get through the museum by killing every guard or, alternatively, by killing no one. Neither of these are goals that Garrett has in the game. There is no in-game way to decide what his goal would be in this respect. The game can be successfully played either way.

To realize this goal of getting through the museum by killing no one, say, you have to make it Garrett's in-game goal, treat it just the way you would his own goals, the goals that you are inhabiting and forced to do (according to claim 1). You must do this, because the world in which Garrett moves allows this goal to be reached in some ways and not others, and it allows it to be reached more easily and effectively (even more elegantly) in some ways than others. This is all thanks to the mesh built into the game among Garrett's mind/body, his goals, and the specifics of the virtual world in which he moves (as designed by the game's designers).

So, we can revise our three-way interaction a bit: we can say now that a video game creates a three-way interaction among the virtual character's mind/body (the player's surrogate), the character's goals and the player's goals, and the virtual world in terms of affordances for effective action:

virtual character ↔ character's goals + player's goals ↔ virtual world.

So, in a video game, players attempt to insert themselves—their own desires, values, and goals—into the mesh. They create, by their play, a mesh among the character (avatar), the character's goals and now their own, too, and the virtual world as it is designed to mesh with the character. When I, Jim, play *Thief: The Deadly Shadows* Garrett becomes me and I become Garrett in that we share goals, some of which are his (imposed on me by him) and some of which are mine (imposed on him by me). And we both must respect the world and how it can or cannot fit well with our actions and goals.

In playing a game, we players are both imposed upon by the character we play (i.e., we must take on the character's goals) and impose ourselves on that character (i.e., we make the character take on our goals). It is interesting to note that this is a theme Bakhtin (1981, 1986) focuses on for language. He uses the term "centripetal force" for my term "being imposed upon" and the term "centrifugal force" for my term, "impose upon". I think there is good reason for this—this symmetry between games and language that we have been arguing for in this book.

Garrett is a project I inherit from the game's designers, and, thus, in that sense an imposition. I had better understand that project (as designed by the game's designers) if I am to carry it out well. But Garrett is also a being into whom I project my own desires, intentions, and goals, but with careful thought about Garrett as a project—that is, once again, with careful thought about the design of the game.

This amounts to saying that both to carry out the Garrett project and to project my desires, intentions, and goals into Garrett, I have to think like a game designer. I have to reflect on and "psych out" the design of the game. This dual nature of game characters as they are played by players—that they are projects the player has been handed and beings into which the players project their desires, intentions, and goals—is why I refer to them as "projective identities", a phrase meant to capture their double-sided nature (Gee 2007). Garrett/Jim is a projective identity, one that is more than Garrett and Jim as separate identities (which they are as well).

There are, then, three identities at play in gaming: There is "Jim", me as a complex real-world person, capable of being many different things in the real world. There is Garrett, a character in a game world with its own universe of discourse (an avatar as body, identity, and tool-kit). And there is the meld "Garrett/Jim" when I take Garrett on as project and project my own desires, values, goals onto and into him, as well (projective identity).

So what?

So what? Who cares that video game characters like Garrett can be projective beings? The double-sided projective nature of video game characters is one of the central sources of the profound pleasures video games offer humans. This is so, I claim, because in the real world we humans receive our deepest pleasure—our most profound feelings of mastery and control—when we can successfully take on what I have called a projective identity in the real world. This is when things really "work" for us.

We all might think that it would be wonderful indeed if the real world was as clear and well designed for each of us as individuals to accomplish our goals as the *Thief* world is for Garrett or the *Mario* world is for Mario. But, alas, it isn't. Life can be tougher and less fair than any video game.

I have said throughout this book that when we humans act and interact in the real world we do so as avatars (social identities). In my own life, I sometimes act as a professor, sometimes as a birder, sometimes as a gamer, sometimes as a father, sometimes as an "everyday person" (an identity we all have, but play out in different ways depending on our culture). Others can be ("play" as) business executives, soldiers, gang members, radical activists, avid runners, bikers, hip-hop artists, lawyers, craftsmen, politicians (all of different types, there are many different ways to be each thing), and so on and so forth.

When I act as a professor, I act in the parts of the world that constitute a professor's reality. I might think: Wouldn't it be nice if that reality, that world, was well designed to fit or mesh with just the sorts of writing, research, and teaching skills I personally have?

Well, in one sense, it would not, in fact be good. Then there would only be one type of successful professor (my type). We would all lose the innovation and productivity we gain from diversity. I would lose the value of colleagues different from me, colleagues who can supplement my weaknesses. I would also lose the opportunity to change into a different type of professor if and when I wanted to.

So the world does not always mesh well with my skills as a professor and that is, perhaps, good, though often frustrating. But, nonetheless, to be a successful professor I have to try to create a mesh between myself and the world, to design, as well as I can, the world around me and myself to fit well together in my attempt to be a professor. This is to say that I must take a projective stance toward or create a projective identity in the real world.

What this means is that first I have to ask what the goals are that are imposed on me, whether I like it or not, as a professor. What are the goals imposed on me by the very nature of the "game" of being a professor. I have to accept this project and try to get the world to mesh with this identity ("professor") and its goals as well as I can. Institutions and social conventions have created a certain sort of mesh between these goals and the world professors inhabit (colleges). As in a good game, there is usually more than one way to accomplish these professor goals and I have to find the ways that I have the abilities to pull off. If I have no such abilities, then I am out of luck. In that case, I can be a professor no more than I can play *Thief* if I am no good at stealth of any kind.

I also have to project onto the identity of being a professor my own desires, values, and goals and see how these can best be accomplished given the constraints on what professors can and cannot do. By projecting onto the professor identity my own desires, values, and goals, I take proactive ownership of that identity and do not view it as a mere imposition. I impose on it, as it imposes on me. We (Jim and the identity "professor") both become something different, a new melded being: Professor/Jim. I fit myself into the mesh:

professor ↔ professor's goals + my goals ↔ real world.

Just as game designers create a game in which there is a certain mesh between character and game world, a mesh that determines the range of ways the game can be played successfully, the social world, with its history and conventions, determines the mesh between a social identity and the real world. This mesh determines the range of ways people can "play" the identity.

Transformation

When you play as Garrett or Solid Snake you make your own Garrett and Snake, but within the constraints of the way the character and the world in which he moves are designed to mesh together for successful action. There are three "players" at play and the three interact. There is the avatar and the possibilities and constraints the avatar brings to the game. There is the human player and the possibilities and constraints the human as an individual with certain desires, values, and abilities brings to the game. And then there is the avatar as a project the player accepts and as the player projects his or her own desires, values, and abilities onto the avatar. That is the projective identity, the avatar/player identity.

But who, for heaven's sake, is a human being? Who is me, Jim? We have seen that each of us is not one thing, but many. We enact different identities in different contexts of our lives. But each of us is also the sum of our identities and our trajectories through life. We are each the intersection of all that we have done and been and are in the process of doing and becoming.

This self which is sum and intersection of our identities and experiences is the "I" that can watch ourselves carry out specific identities at different times and still see each performance as "me". This is the "I" that can tell our own personal tale, a tale that, however loosely or complexly, attempts to knit together all our identities and performances into some bigger story. If people cannot tell such a story—if they cannot feel an "I" behind all the other "I's" that carry out specific roles, actions, and identities—they get sick in mind and often body too. They have no sense of self.

Let's call this storied, partially unified, "I" (the one behind and composed of all its experiences and identities) the "self". It takes work to attempt to unify a self, to feel true connection between all the experiences and identities in our lives. It is a project that is never finished and can go awry. Our self can tatter and even shatter. We can change our story of self in small or large ways or life can force such changes on us. But most of humans need, want, and attempt to have a self.

A video game player is a self. When I play I bring my whole history and my various other identities to bear. I can call on them as resources and possibilities and they set some limitations on me as a player. That is why, in the last chapter, my analysis of *Metal Gear Solid 4: Guns of the Patriots* is so influenced by the fact that I am old and other related things.

When a gamer plays as Garrett or Snake there are limitations on how much they can shape these characters to their own desires and purposes. Garrett could not beat Riddick in an open fight and Snake does not have a flamethrower.

However, gamers can, if they learn how, "mod" games. They can use software that often comes with a game or is otherwise accessible to modify the game in small or large ways. They can turn *Thief* into a fighting game and give Snake a flamethrower and go all Rambo. They could even make *Grand Theft Auto* a game about taking photographs rather than shooting people, about replacing goods rather than stealing them, and about investing in prostitutes' education rather than sleeping with them. They could—I am getting carried away here—put Chibi-Robo into *Grand Theft Auto* so he could clean and make people happy. That's the magic of programming and programming today is more user-friendly and more accessible to players than ever before.

In our lives we are stuck with avatars society has given us. I cannot be a male, a lover, a citizen, a professor in any old way I want. Society has set up conventions and expectations and institutions that enforce them. I can project my desires, values, and goals onto my real-life avatars, but within the constraints of how society "wants" that avatar to mesh with the world for success.

But can we "mod" real life? Can we change the character of the real-life avatars and games we play? The answer is yes, but we have to put in the effort, learning, and risk of failure and humiliation. The consequences are bigger than in playing and modding video games. But we can use the resources that our experiences in life and our other identities have given us to proactively work for change. If we take the risk and modify the game and we succeed in the sense that people allow it, recognize it, and get influenced by it, we can change the game for everyone forever.

The avatar "husband" was designed by society to mesh with the world only in terms of a male marrying a woman playing the avatar "wife". Now men marry men and women marry women. New avatars have arisen and the game has changed.

Gays modded the institution of marriage based on an assessment of the modern world and possibilities for change. They played within the rules in many respects (e.g., by demanding legal marriages), but changed them in the process. Their tools for modding were collaboration, risk taking, innovation, persisting past failure, creating new language, and engaging politics and institutions as activists. They are not finished, the battle is not totally won. There have been costs—dead bodies on fence posts—but there has been and will be yet more gains for all of us in society.

I am an old heterosexual man who has always seen marriage as a pointless, too constraining, statist institution. It was never an avatar or game I wanted to play. As I watched gays mod the game and saw the new meanings they were giving it and the old meanings they were reinvigorating, I stood in a creek in my hometown of Sedona, Arizona and married the woman I will die with. All of sudden it was a game I wanted to play and a new avatar I wanted to take on.

12

AVATARS AND BIG "D" DISCOURSES

Avatars and conversations

In the last chapter we used games to look at avatars in games and in real life. We argued that in both games and real life humans have to find and help shape a mesh between themselves, their avatar, and the game or real world.

In this chapter we look at talk to see how avatars work in the real world and how avatars are learned and constructed through conversations. The conversation printed below is from a mathematics class. The class is being taught by Maggie Lampert, a professor of mathematics education at the University of Michigan, but also a fifth-grade math teacher. The data below is from one of Lampert's fifth-grade classes. It is from an introductory lesson on functions (Lampert, et al. 1996; see also Lampert 2001 for Lampert's views on teaching mathematics).

The discussion below occurred in a whole-class discussion after small-group work. Several of the small groups had found the following problem difficult: Given four sets of number pairs, what is the rule to get from the first number to the second? The number pairs were 8–4, 4–2, 2–1, and 0–0. Below, Lampert is the teacher and the other names are the names of students. We start mid-stream in the discussion (I will say below why some parts are bolded and some in italics):

1 Ellie:	Um, well, there were a whole bunch of—a whole bunch of rules you could use, use, um, divided by two—And you could do, um, minus one-half.	
2 Lampert:	And eight minus a half is?	
3 Ellie:	Four. [In response to this answer, audible gasps can be heard from the class, and several other students tried to enter the conversation.]	

ert: You think that would be four. **What does somebody else think?**

I, I started raising a question because a number of people have a different idea about that. So let's hear what your different ideas are and see if you can take Ellie's position into consideration and try to let her know what your position is. Enoyat?

Well, see, *I agree with Ellie* because you can have eight minus one half and that's the same as eight divided by two or eight minus four.

Eight divided by two is four, eight minus four is four? Okay, **so Enoyat thinks he can do all of those things to eight and get four**. Okay? Charlotte?

Um, I think eight minus one half is seven and a half because—

Why?

Um, one half's a fraction and it's a half of one whole and so when you subtract you aren't even subtracting one whole number so you can't get even a smaller number that's more than one whole. *But I see what Ellie's doing*, she's taking half the number she started with and getting the answer.

;o, you would say one half of eight? Is that what you
ıean?

ampert and Charlotte alternate for three turns; then, Lampert 'ecks in with Ellie, who again repeats her original answer; ·n Lampert calls on Shakroukh.]

'ould agree with Ellie if she had added something else to her ılanation, if she had said one-half of the amount that you ɛ to divide by two.

ıy. You guys are on to something really important ıt fractions, which is that a fraction is a fraction of ething. And we have to have some kind of agree-...ent here if it's a fraction of eight or if it's a fraction of a whole.

How we talk about and use mathematics is determined by what sort of mathematical avatar we are enacting. There are many different ways to do, value, think about, and act with mathematics in the world. Pure mathematicians, applied mathematicians, architects, engineers (of various sorts), programmers, and others talk, act, think, and value differently in the world when using mathematics. They "play" different games with it, that is, they engage in different practices with mathematics. In each such game, they have to be and act out different kinds of people valuing, using, thinking about, and acting with mathematics in different ways with different goals.

When a child is learning mathematics in school—as these children are—they might very well be asking themselves questions like: Why should I want to do this?

What can I do and be with it? Who else does it and why? These are all good questions. If I told you that you were going to take complex lessons on standing on your head and walking on your arms, you would be asking the very same questions and probably would not learn well or even participate if I did not come up with some good answers.

Very often the avatar for doing mathematics at school—for playing the game of "school math"—is as a memorizer of facts and formulas and a test passer. That is why one sort of standard conversational format in school math classes is a set of "IRE" (Initiation, Response, Evaluation) sequences, as below (data is made up):

Teacher to group:	What is 8 minus one-half?
One Student or Several:	7 and one half.
Teacher:	Correct.
Teacher:	How did you get that answer?
Student/s:	I subtracted ½ of 1 from 8.
Teacher:	Great. You've got it.

This very conversational format—which can, of course, be played out in many different ways with variations—represents quite clearly that math is answering questions about facts and formulas in a test-like why. In some classrooms this is pretty much what it means to do mathematics and be a "good math student" (an avatar). Of course, in these classrooms there are other formats for talk, action, and interaction, but many of them reinforce the same message.

Lampert is engaging the students in a very different sort of conversation. She is introducing her students to a different game with a different sort of avatar. I have bolded the parts of Lampert's talk that are types of "meta talk". She is asking the children to think about thinking and to pay attention to what things mean. She is also stressing mathematics as interactions among people who think about what other students have said, what they meant, and why they said what they did. They do this so that when they respond to other students they can build on what these other students have done, either by correcting it, supplementing it, or improving upon it.

In Lampert's class, mathematics is collaborative, accumulative (builds knowledge by building on each other's talk and ideas), and reflects about how thinking works and what things mean. Even wrong answers, when reflected on, can show a certain sense and correctness and clarify the path forward.

The students are getting two answers not because some of them are "slow", but because they are coming to realize that "eight minus a half is?"—Lampert's question—has two different interpretations. It can mean "What is eight minus ½ of 1?" or it can mean "What is eight minus ½ of itself?". Lampert is making clear that in doing mathematics and being a certain sort of mathematician you need to come to agreements about how to talk and what things mean (these are sometimes in math called "stipulations") in more explicit ways than you often have to do in everyday life using everyday language.

So, in the classroom, via such orchestrated conversations, students are learning that the avatar of doing mathematics (playing that game) in this classroom involves things like paying close attention to other students (not just the teacher), orienting to those students, collaborating, tying to and building on previous talk, accumulating knowledge, coming to agreements, learning shared ways of using language in a special domain, and thinking about thinking and meaning. This is the identity, body, and tools children inherit in this sort of mathematics class and in this construal of what mathematics is as a "game", activity, or form of life in the world. In the transcript above I have placed in italics some students' comments that demonstrate in talk this orientation.

Lampert sets mathematics up as this sort of "game" with this sort of "avatar" because she believes that it allows students to find a mesh between themselves, this new identity, and the world of mathematics that is meaningful and participatory and ties to a number of different domains in the real world where mathematics is used (that is, sets up possible transfer to those domains). This approach will prepare students to be able to learn in later domains (like programming, engineering, digital art, and so forth) that use mathematics, should they be motivated to do so.

Of course, we have looked at but one small moment in Lampert's class and only one of her activities. Nonetheless, I hope it is clear how conversation in this class—conversation of a certain sort—introduces students through action and interaction to mathematics as a specific game or world in which people act, talk, and value in certain ways. Some of these ways are set by the conventions and rules mathematicians follow and some are open to students finding their own personal goals and ways of succeeding within the constraints set by the "game". There are even opportunities for modding in a classroom like this, as students teach each other, help design curricula, and come to agreements and new collaborations with each other.

The IRE conversation and Lampert's conversation are two different games with two different avatars. They invite students to do mathematics and be mathematicians in quite different ways. But they both enact mathematics as a conversation with others and with the world of numbers.

Affordances

In the IRE math "game", talk is an affordance for assessing one's ability to answer test like questions and to get assessed by the teacher in those terms. The effective abilities required are knowing the answers and being able to answer the questions.

In Lampert's math game, talk is an affordance for collaboratively co-designing solutions to math problems and reflecting on mathematical thinking and reasoning in one's self and in others. The effective abilities required are social, interactive, and meta-cognitive.

In the IRE game, failure does not teach anyone much and leads to embarrassment. In Lampert's class failure leads to learning as it is explored, reflected on, and used for fodder for understanding, seeing what things can mean, and moving forward as an individual and a group. Failure need not be an embarrassment. Indeed, it can sometimes be seen as a success when looked at in a different way (What is eight minus half of eight?). Looking at things in multiple ways and paying close attention to different interpretations is a great way to gain meta-knowledge and even a great way to help facilitate innovation.

Lampert is aware that avatars as identities, skills, and tools are built in conversations with others and with the world. They are built in conversations which are reflective and responsive and turn taking, the sorts of conversations we have argued that are fundamental to discourse analysis, to games, to science, and to life.

Discourses with a big "D"

I have so far called games "games" and said that game play is a type of reciprocal and responsive conversation. I have sometimes metaphorically called conversations with other people (who I treat as worlds) and with the real world "games" with "avatars". In earlier work I used a different term. I used the term "Discourse" with a capital "D" (Gee 2011, 2014a, 2014b). In that work I used "discourse" with a little "d" to mean stretches of talk or text, language in use in context.

Big D Discourses are ways to enact and recognize socially meaningful identities. They are ways to "talk the talk" and "walk the walk" to enact identities like being a "tough cop", a "hip African-American", a "real Indian" (a term used by some Native-Americans), an anime otaku, an "old middle-class white baby-boomer" (each of a certain sort), and many many more. They are the sorts of "talking the talk" and "walking the walk" by which other people recognize such identities in order to interact with them, contest them, learn them, or be them.

A Discourse requires a person to act, interact, value, and dress in certain ways and not others. It is an identity, a body with certain skills and ways of being used, and a tool-kit. It is what we have called an avatar. History, society, and conventions determine the possible avatars at any one time, though people can transform them and mod them within certain constraints.

Game designers design avatars (thus, playing the role played by history, society, and conventions in real-life Discourses) and we players play them. We talk their talk and walk their walk as we play, though, here too, we can transform them and mod them within certain constraints. Games are mini-Discourses, ways of acting, interacting, and valuing in order to enact and recognize a given identity, whether this be Solid Snake, a solider in *Call of Duty*, or a house-cleaning happiness robot. Games are great in part because they add Discourses to the world and let us play with and within them.

Discourses are the stuff that constitutes our human social, cultural, and institutional worlds—they are the sea we swim in as social beings—and so games are playing with the very stuff of life. Both life and games are doing and being and, importantly, marriages of the two: being something by doing things in certain ways and doing things in certain ways because we are being something, being something that at least some others recognize.

Why the word (with a capital) "Discourse"? I use this term because in history and society it is not just individual people like me and you that talk and act. We talk and act as something, in the guise of a certain recognizable identity. These identities—things like Anglo-Americans, African-Americans, Native-Americans, policemen, soldiers, gamers, birders, lawyers, activists, feminists, "new males", and Wall Street bankers (all of these have different types)—are historical kinds of people talking to and acting each other through history. That is what constitutes society.

When we talk and act as individuals we talk and act both as personal individuals and as historical kinds of people. We produce and reproduce historically recognizable kinds of people—that is, Discourses—through time. Discourses talk to each other across time and space, just as individuals do, and they use us individuals to do so.

Think about the long-running conversations between police and gangs (of different types), between biologists and creationists, between liberals and conservatives, between socialists and capitalists, between towns and gowns, corporations and environmentalists, between teachers and students. And, of course, these conversations are not always just two-way. Often there are many different Discourses in the conversation. For example, consider "global warming" (better "man-made climate change") as a conversation. The Discourses of different sorts of scientists, activists, corporations, government officials, and various media all interact to shape this conversation.

Discourses are ways of thinking, believing, valuing, acting, interacting, dressing, gesturing, and using objects, tools, technologies, places, spaces, and times to enact or pull off a socially recognizable identity or avatar. They begin and end in history, change and transform as they live, and their interactions with each other across time and space constitute history and society. They need us to carry them through space and time, just as video games need players.

We are each parts of many different Discourses. Maybe you are a certain sort of African-American, Evangelical Christian, middle manager, avid marathon runner, citizen scientist with a telescope contributing to astronomy (perhaps, you do *Galaxy Zoo*), and a member of the local school board and a local politician. Each of your identities constrains what you can say, do, and be in certain ways if you want to be recognized and accepted in that identity.

However, you can let aspects of your different Discourses influence each other. If you do this—say you let aspects of your African-American Church Discourse influence how you act, interact, and talk in your Politician Discourse—then if you are still recognized and accepted in the Politician Discourse, you have made a bid to change it.

This is what Jesse Jackson did at the national level. He got enough people to still see him as a national politician even though he integrated aspects of his African-American Church Discourse (he was a minister) into his mainstream Politician Discourse. He did not win, but he got enough acceptance to pave the way for many other African-American politicians to win and use aspects of their other Discourses for success in their political careers. In fact, today even some White politicians use rhetorical devices rooted in African-American churches in their speeches.

Of course, letting one Discourse influence another is a risk. It is a bid to get recognized by melding the old and new and can fail. Many a student has found that trying to meld rhetorical aspects of their African-American Discourse into school essays does not always work. The School Essayist Discourse often resists changes, partly because it is nearly moribund in the world outside of school and often used in schools more for sorting and test purposes than as a future powerful resource for students.

So we can talk about the Solid Snake Discourse (ways of doing/being Solid Snake), the Zelda Discourse (ways of doing/being characters in the Zelda universe of discourse), the tough-guy biker Discourse (ways of doing/being a tough-guy biker), the Special Ed Student Discourse, the fundamentalist Christian Discourse, the Wall Street Financier Discourse, the ADHD Discourse, the Birder Discourse, and so on and so forth through the whole human tapestry of history and society.

Discourses can appear and disappear. In the Middle Ages there was no way really to get recognized as a schizophrenic. No medical Discourses existed yet that could support such an identity. However, St. Simeon Stylites (see: http://www.newadvent. org/cathen/13795a.htm) spent the last years of his life living on a small platform on top of a pillar and got recognized as a saint (actually, compared to other aspects of his life, this may have been the least odd thing he did). Today he would get recognized as having some sort of mental illness. You cannot be a dyslexic in a society that has no reading and it is hard to be one in a society that writes but not with an alphabet (alphabets match sounds and letters). Some children may have a learning disability at school but not at home. Their Learning Disabled Discourse is only played out at school (McDermott 1993).

None of this means Discourses are not "real". However, humans have a great many traits and these traits can be recruited in different ways by different Discourses. What is a lack of focus in one Discourse may be multi-tasking in another. What is a too obsessively narrow focus in one Discourse may be a specialist skill in another Discourse. What is criminal in one Discourse may be social activism in another (e.g., hacking). A terrorist in one Discourse may be seen as a freedom fighter in another. But how we get recognized is deeply consequential in society and the real world.

We have argued that avatars in video games are in reality three related things: a body (ways of being and skill and abilities), an identity, and a tool-kit. But this is just what constitutes a Discourse. A Discourse tells us how to do, be, and what tools to use.

When you go to that tough biker bar or that bank boardroom meeting, you better have the right body and skills, the right identity, and the right tools. Bikers bring jeans and jackets, not suits. They sit at the bar not the boardroom table. They have to know how to talk and act tough, not how to talk and act rich, and they bring bikes and knives with them, not fancy cars and lawyers. Both have been known to carve other people up, just in quite different ways.

13

READING

Non-responsive media

Print and literary criticism

In this book I have argued that conversation is the primordial form of human communication. I mean conversations with other people and with the world. This primordial form has now been extended to conversations with game worlds.

As Plato already knew (Gee 2011), this leaves written language (and things like film) as problematic. Books and movies can't talk back. They cannot take their turns. When we interrogate them, they stay silent.

So what to make of these mute forms? To understand a book readers must carry on conversations with themselves in their heads. They have to ask the questions and answer them themselves. And this can be a problematic process.

The field of literary criticism has long been vexed by the issue of who literary texts are addressed to and which readers count as "competent" to read them. Written language, just like oral language, has to be recipiently designed. Its sentences have to be designed to seek or anticipate a particular response. Its sentences have to be addressed to some type of reader. Literary critics call this the "implied reader" (Iser 1974).

This is so because the syntax of language exists in part to package what we say in ways that address others and seek or anticipate a particular response from them. If writers did not know who they were addressing and what responses they wanted, they would not know how to design their sentences. Emily Dickinson wrote "My life closed twice, before its close" as the first line of one of her poems. Why didn't she write "Before its close, my life closed twice"? Or "My life, before its close, closed twice" or "Twice my life closed, before its close"?

Why did she write in poetry and not prose? Dickinson's poems are written in the meter of the Protestant Hymnal at a time where everyone in town (Amherst, Massachusetts) was Christian (Morgan 2010). Yet her poems often engage in heretical thoughts (e.g., "Parting is all we know of heaven, and all we need of hell"). Why, then, did she write in a meter associated with church?

Should Emily Dickinson's poems be read in terms of the people who lived in her place and time? Which ones of them? Should they be read in terms of people who live now? Which ones of them? Are they meant just for "professional" poetry readers? Just for other poets? Then or now?

Literary criticism has dealt poorly with these issues. It has too often pretended that literary works are addressed to some "universal reader" (there are none) or "competent reader", where "competent" often means having been trained in whatever is at the time the dominant trend in English departments (Chatman 1978, 1990).

There are no universal readers or writers because, as we have seen, humans communicate in terms of identities (avatars). We have to know who Emily Dickinson is speaking as and who she thinks she is speaking to. Literary critics call this the "implied author" (Booth 2005). Is Dickinson writing as a Christian, a heretic, a woman, a lesbian, a lover, a recluse, a nineteenth-century poet, a New Englander, or something else or some meld of these?

Given that her heretical thoughts are put in the meter of the Hymnal, is she addressing Christians, religious skeptics, or people who have doubts in the middle of the night? Is she speaking to "souls" with which she feels kinship as a reclusive religiously skeptical lesbian poet writing at a time when women's freedom of thought and action was quite restricted?

Reading as a conversation

When we read something we must respond to the text in our heads and then we must respond back to ourselves for the text, since it cannot talk. We read a bit and then we respond, consciously or unconsciously in our heads. We ask a question, make a comment, express agreement or disagreement, threaten to stop reading, or beg for more. Then we imagine what response the text could make.

We have seen that all language engages with recipient design. All language is designed to get or anticipate a response when the other takes his or her turn. We have also seen that all language is action. Just like in conversations with the world, where we act and pay attention to the world's response, conversations in language, whether with people or texts, are actions intended to get a response from the listener. Speakers attempt to get the hearer to do or feel something. Writers want to get readers to do or feel something, as well.

So readers have to ask what this text is trying to do to them. What response does it want? Does it want me to respond only in my mind or in the world? After all, many a sacred text has been read as a call to action, sometimes actions to make the world better and sometimes violent actions to kill "unbelievers".

And here is the biggest problem with written texts: When we respond, take our turn, we have to answer our own responses. We have to "speak for" the text and its author. And the temptation will always be to answer in ways that just support what we already believe. Humans have a "confirmation bias" in terms of which they are much better at seeking and finding confirmations of their own views than they are at challenging those views.

Reading can become an echo chamber in which we bend texts to our own beliefs, values, and desires, or, if we cannot, reject them. We can read Emily Dickinson as a good Christian church woman (she was no such thing). We can read her poems as "cute" little ditties written by and for women (they were no such thing—she is as nasty as William Blake).

The fact that books make readers engage in both sides of a conversation is one of the reasons why literacy has very often not been all that liberating. In fact, often the most educated and literate people in a society are the most politically quiescent, the ones who trust and buy into the status quo the most.

So what is to be done?

Readers as double selves

We saw at the outset of this book that humans can play video games in their heads. They can role play as themselves and others in worlds they imagine. So readers can interrogate a text—respond to it—in terms of one of their real-world identities (say, in my case, as elderly professor opposed to neoliberalism) and answer back in terms of another one of their identities (say, in my case, a person with lots of class rage) or in terms of an identity they can imagine as appropriate to the writer and his or her text (e.g., as a free-thinking woman living amidst oppression at a time when few people will fully recognize her poetry). That is, we can set up a dialogue in our heads.

Reading this way means that texts can be read many ways and many times if they really serve as good fodder for good "talk" in our heads and with other people out in the world. This does not mean that texts can be read any way we want. If we are to be fair, we have to imagine an identity (avatar, "implied author") for authors that honor what seems to be their intentions, given how they have designed (packaged) their sentences. But this is true also of oral conversation. We have to honor what others have said and how they have said it as people who share a language with us. Emily Dickinson's poem "My Life Closed Twice" is not about ice-cream. We have to treat writers as if they have spoken and spoken out of a specific identity (avatar).

Affordances

The conversation we set up in our heads when we read is one between one of our real-life identities (or an imagined identity) and an identity we have (fairly) imagined for the writer based on how he or she has designed the sentences in the text. Note, too, that written language has no intonation—no pitch, tone, and stress of the voice—as oral language does. So readers must add this. They must say in their heads what writers have written. They must add the intonation. They must "voice" the text out loud or in their heads.

English uses intonation to signal affect and to foreground and background information, among other things, and so without any intonation we cannot know crucial things about meaning. So, quite literally, we turn written language into oral language in our heads. We take on the moral responsibility of speaking for the writer, of voicing his or her words. And we have also to respond (as ourselves) to those worlds and then make up (imagine) a response on the author's part. In this sense, reading is also "writing" as we extend texts by adding responses to our questions that we imagine the author (or implied author) of the text would give.

Writing leads back to voice and to turn-taking conversations. If we ask and answer only as ourselves and our beliefs we create an echo chamber. If we set up a dialogue between or among different identities (some of our own and imagined ones for ourselves and the author), then we can learn something and have something more to say to others.

Emily Dickinson, "Parting"

When we look at language as action, we have to ask who a text thinks we are (what identity or avatar is being addressed) and what it is trying to do to us. Then we have to respond by talking back to the text (and, then, imagine its reply). Let's look for a minute at Emily Dickinson's poem "Parting":

My life closed twice before its close—
It yet remains to see
If Immortality unveil
A third event to me

So huge, so hopeless to conceive
As these that twice befell.
Parting is all we know of heaven,
And all we need of hell.

One way I read this poem is as a former devout Catholic who worried a good deal about heaven and hell. I read Dickinson as addressing a Protestant Christian world that worried greatly about deeds and riches as signs that meant they were worthy of going to heaven and not to hell. These were people who lived in fear that, no matter what they did, they might not be "chosen".

I read Dickinson as engaged in the following actions: She wants to suggest that heaven and hell are here on earth and not in some after-life. She wants readers to live their lives here and now in the present world and not in anticipation and dread of another after-life world.

I agree with this sentiment, though I know what it would be like to oppose it via my former devout Catholic identity. However, I have a response to Dickinson: Why even use the words "heaven" and "hell"? For that matter, why write in the meter of the Protestant Hymnal. Why use religious language at all? Why not free ourselves from the whole thing, dismissing it as a matter of superstition?

Now, I can stop there and learn nothing from the poem. But if I search for an answer to my questions from the point of view of some identity I imagine Emily Dickinson as having written out of, I can have a good conversation from which I might learn something.

Here is one answer I can give: Dickinson is saying (see how I am now speaking for her) that there are truths in religious beliefs, but not the ones most religious people see. We humans do have souls that in some sense transcend our bodies. Since religious people believe this, they imagine that when the body dies, the soul lives on and must therefore live on in some world. Some cultures might believe the soul lives on in this world as a "spirit" or "ghost". But Christians believe it lives on in an after-life where it reaps its just rewards (or is just fortunate enough to have been chosen, for those who do not believe in "works").

Emily, however, is suggesting that there is a part of each human that cannot die the way the body can. The body can be horribly traumatized only once and then dies and that is the end of pain. But there is a part of humans—an emotional part—that can be horribly traumatized over and over again until the body dies. This part of us does not die when it is "killed". It lives on to "die" again, until our body dies. If I stab your body hard enough you die, but I can stab your soul over and over again.

Given that Emily believes this, she is also suggesting that if this soul part of us could not suffer such huge pain it could not also enjoy such huge joy. No big lows, no big highs. The highs—the loves gained—are all we are going to get of heaven and so we better fully live them. The lows—the loves lost—are all we need of hell, because without them there could be no moments of transcendent joy, so we must not fear hell, but allow for it.

This emotional part of humans is still mysterious to science. How do we humans exist as beings conscious of life and death, capable of foul deeds and wondrous altruism? How can anyone suffer the loss of a child and live on? How can anyone not feel the joy of real love as something to treasure fully and now?

Emily's poem taught me that "emotion" is a much less good word than "soul" for this part of each of us that dies many times before we die, if we are truly living now and not just for the next life. It also makes me see how deeply sad it is when any human being does not get an opportunity to risk and live life in full. Dickinson's poem is indeed a hymn worth singing, especially when we hear whispers of mortality in the dark of night and fear retribution for our weaknesses.

So I am reading Emily Dickinson here as a former devout Catholic old enough to see death on the horizon. I hear her speaking to me as an outsider in her time and place who sought sense in what others believed, but rejected their fears of life, bodies, love, and difference.

There are many other fruitful readings of Dickinson's poem. There are as many as there are fair construals of who Emily was (like all of us she had multiple identities) and who she was writing as. And, indeed, writing is great when it sets up multiple good conversations.

Note, too, that what I have done is recruit effective abilities I possess in order to use affordances I see in the poem to accomplish my goals in reading. My goals in this case are appreciation of poetry as a form of voice and a desire to make more sense of what I found good and what I found bad in religion. I also want to understand how Emily (if I can call her that) lived. I want to understand why she became a recluse and yet wrote poetry that was not the voice of mental illness, but of profound mental health. The effective abilities I bring to the poem—and therefore the affordances in it I can use—stem from the skills I have developed in reading theology, reading poetry only late in life and never in school, and in having written about style in poetry as a linguist. Others bring other effective abilities and take up other affordances. That is why it is always useful for people to share interpretations of writing, to expose their multiple and diverse conversations.

Creating worlds

Earlier in this book I said that when we interact with a game world or the real world with goals in mind, we have to use X-ray vision. We have to see through irrelevant details and aspects of the world to the details and aspects that are relevant to us for accomplishing our goals. We have to simplify the richness of the world, to pay attention to, to focus on, the right parts.

Often when we speak to others or interact with the world, we are faced with a replete and rich context. When we talk to others we can see them, question them, and often know something about them. When we interact with the real world or a game world, we see and are inside the world (in game, we are in the game world thanks to our surrogate body, our avatar). So we usually have to subtract irrelevant details from the context and focus only on the aspects of the context relevant to our interpretation and our goals.

Writing very often comes with much less context and no opportunity to ask the text more about itself. In writing, we often have to imagine in our heads the larger world or context which gives the text its situated meanings, deeper interpretations, and relevance. Rather than having to subtract irrelevant details, as we often do in game play and in interacting in and with the real world, we have to add relevant details that may not be explicitly discussed in the text.

Now, I want to note that there are types of speech that are like writing and contextually impoverished and not highly responsive (e.g., lectures, especially ones video-taped for e-learning). And there are types of writing that are more contextually rich (e.g., personal letters and notes at home to family members). Nonetheless, much of the writing we see and do in the modern world is contextually impoverished and non-responsive.

For example, say you were reading about the causes of death across the world and came across this sentence: "Many children die in Africa before they are five years old because they contract infectious diseases like malaria". This sentence has no real contextual meaning because we do not have a world to go with it. It is about the real world, but does not give us enough of the real world to know what details are relevant to interpreting it.

What is the appropriate amount of context that we should imagine in our minds in order to understand and assess this claim? We could consider just medical facts, a narrow context. And in that context all that seems relevant is the truth that viruses and bacteria can and do kill. Of course, this does not tell us why it is African kids that are dying so often and so young. And, indeed, this is a question we might very well want to put to the text, though we will have to answer it for ourselves in the absence of any more information.

We could widen the medical context, though still stay within only medical aspects of the world. We could say to ourselves, this sentence means something like "Many children die in Africa before they are five years old because they contract infectious diseases like malaria and do not have access to immunization and necessary medicines". This still begs the question of why they do not have access to these medical necessities. Perhaps, we will feel that it is because drug companies price the drugs too high, or some other reason due to medical delivery systems.

We could widen the context beyond medicine and consider aspects of the real world like poverty. We might then add in the fact that almost all deaths from infectious diseases occur in the non-industrialized world where poverty affects not just how people die, but how they live. Poor people have less good health than rich people and their lack of good health affects what eventually kills them.

Each of these different ways of adding in relevant details changes the nature and meaning of causation and blame we attribute to the claim in the sentence. We can go on to say that it is poverty and poor access to health care that actually causes the death and viruses and bacteria just serve as an agent.

This still leaves the question as to why Africa is poor and why it has poor access to modern medicine. Here we can think about such details as colonization, history, global economics, drug pricing, various forms of capitalism, and the history of race.

So while in verbal conversations with other people and with the real world and game worlds, we often have to subtract from too rich information to focus on the relevant details, in writing we often have to add richer details to the writing in order to create the relevant details necessary to understand the text, respond to it, or use it for our purposes.

So just as we have to take both sides of the conversation when reading and respond for the text, we also have to supply aspects of the world relevant to the text that have been left out (and no text can say everything explicitly; all texts must leave much to be inferred by readers). It is not that we do not make guesses and inferences when we talk to others, but we can in that case check the guesses and inferences and we usually start with a far richer setting or context.

Writing is somewhat like yeast. It is a starter for or fodder for conversations that readers carry out in their own heads or in conversations about the texts with other people. Note, too, that in the case of Emily Dickinson's poem, I had to add in a world of nineteenth-century Protestant Christianity and gender relations. Other readers might well have read the poem in terms of another sort of context or world (e.g., the history of poetry or assumptions about "great souls" that transcend culture and history or the world of literary critics reading literature as in need of no context other than its own words).

Texts can, of course, give us more or less information, but they can never say everything relevant to their interpretation and they can never convey the wealth of detail our senses give us of others, the real world, or game worlds.

Let's consider one real example of written language where the context we imagine for it matters a good deal. Consider the statement below about the Annenberg Institute for School Reform at Brown University (http://annenberg institute.org/):

> A national policy research and reform-support organization that works with urban districts and communities to improve the conditions and outcomes of schools, especially in urban communities and in those attended by tradition-ally underserved children. Our work focuses on three crucial issues in edu-cation reform today: school transformation, college and career readiness, and expanded learning time.

This seems unimpeachable and, indeed, the Institute is a worthwhile organization. However, how we add in contexts from the real world will greatly affect how we assess this statement, how we respond to it, and how we carry on a double-sided conversation in our heads about it.

It is very common today to talk and write as if some school reform or another will solve the problems with our schools and improve them for all children. These statements very rarely take into overt consideration the society in which schools exist.

We have known for decades now from research that out of school factors (like poverty, number of books in the home, amount of talk between children and parents, etc.) swamp in-school factors (e.g., small classroom, experienced teachers, good teaching practices, etc.). Both sorts of factors matter and can make a differ-ence, but out-of-school factors matter more in terms of which students succeed and why some poor and minority children fare poorly in school (Gee 2004; Pearson 1997).

We also today have a society in the United States with massive amounts of inequality. Four hundred families own 60 percent of the wealth in the country. We have larger inequality today than at almost any other time in our history. Poor children and families—and many middle class ones—have poor health and poor access to medical care compared to people in other developed countries. Social mobility is higher today in many European countries than it is in the United States. Furthermore, inequality is growing and corporations and Wall Street have a dis-proportionate amount of power and influence on the government (see Ferguson 2012; Frank 2011; Frank 2012; Smith 2012; Stiglitz 2012 for these horrors and many more).

School reformers rarely think about the fact that not any society will accept any type of schools. Will a society as unequal and as dominated by the rich as ours accept, for instance, schools in which all children, rich and poor, learn equally and have the same opportunity to go to elite colleges? Will it spend the resources necessary to make this happen, especially when this would require ameliorating poverty and segregation in society (and not just funding schools fairly) to counter out-of-school factors? Indeed, in response to the 2008 financial crisis, we bailed out banks, but cut social programs.

The statement above talks about "college and career readiness" as one of three issues crucial to school reform. But what does it mean to prepare students for college when most of them will not be able to afford it, certainly not at the most elite institutions? Indeed, today American college students and graduates carry a massive debt load second only to mortgage debt in the United States.

What does it mean to ready students for careers, when the majority of jobs in the United States are low-paying service jobs, Wal-Mart is the biggest employer in the country, and pay and benefits for all sorts of jobs have deteriorated as we have destroyed unions and lowered worker pay and benefits while increasing worker productivity? Is the goal of school really to prepare most students to work in jobs that do not pay a living wage?

Why are all those details of the real world not relevant enough to the text to have been foregrounded in it? Well, in a sense, they are, because by adding them in I just made them relevant and, after all, reading this text is a double-sided conversation in my own mind. It is my conversation.

You may very well add in different aspects of the real world as relevant. You will carry out a different conversation in your head. We might then be prepared to talk to each other and to school reformers. Reading is, at its best, preparation for conversations with others (e.g., about school reform) and with the world (e.g., in reforming society and schools).

Conclusion

The unified theory of discourse analysis we have been developing in this book takes interactive, response-based, turn-taking conversations as the fundamental form of human communication and action in and with the world. We can talk to others and we can talk to worlds and others are, in fact, worlds.

Non-responsive forms like writing, painting, and film are secondary forms. They are parasitic on conversation and demand that readers or viewers carry on, consciously or unconsciously a double-sided conversation with themselves. In this double-sided conversation readers and viewers talk back for the text, film, or painting. They also take the text, film, or painting as the yeast for imagining a larger world within which the reader or viewer can find relevant details to use to situate the meanings of the text, film, or painting, within which to interpret it.

Secondary does not mean less important. It just means that these non-responsive forms have come later and built on what came before. At their best, texts, films, and paintings have added great conversations to the world and made each of us smarter and better by fueling debate, dialogue, and conversations in our own heads as we play out different identities and, perhaps, discover new ways of being in the world and new values and beliefs. At their worst, texts, films, and paintings can just tell us what to believe or reinforce our own beliefs and values as we just repeat what they have already said or seek out only ones that confirm our own biases.

14

ALIGNMENT AND DEVELOPMENT

Conversations

In this book, I have treated conversations as response-sensitive, turn-taking encounters between an actor and a world. In a conversation between two people, the speaker acts on the listener as a complex world. Then they switch roles and the person who was a world acts (speaks) and the other person becomes a world.

Speaking is a form of acting. Speakers seek to inform, convince, motivate, blame, accuse, promise, invite, encourage, or to get the hearer to act in some way. The hearer is a complex world in the sense that he or she is made up of many interacting variables, a system within which speakers must find affordances for accomplishing goals.

Speakers formulate what they say in ways that anticipate a certain response based on the person they are communicating with. This is what linguists call "recipient design". Speakers design what they say based on assumptions (hypotheses) they make about the listener and how they want the listener to respond. After the listener responds, the original speaker must, on his or her next turn, take that response into consideration in formulating a new turn at talk.

Playing a video game is a form of acting. Players seek to accomplish goals. They treat the game world as a complex, designed world made up of interacting variables, a system within which they must find affordances for accomplishing goals. Players formulate what they are going to do based on anticipating and hoping for a certain response from the game. This, too, can be seen as a form of "recipient design". Players design their actions based on assumptions (hypotheses) they make about the game world and the way they want that world to respond. After the game responds, the player must, on his or her next turn, take that response into consideration in formulating a new turn at play.

Doing science is a form of acting. Scientists seek to accomplish goals. They treat the real world as a complex system of interacting variables, a system within which scientists must find affordances for accomplishing (knowledge building) goals. Scientists formulate what they are going to do based on anticipating and hoping for a certain response from the world. This, too, can be seen as a form of "recipient design". Scientists design what they do based on assumptions (hypotheses) they make about the real world and the way they want that world to respond. When the world responds, the scientist must, on his or her next turn, take that response into consideration in formulating a new turn at inquiry.

The world is so complex that scientists often do experiments in laboratories, test models, or use simulations. In this case they are acting on—interrogating—artificial worlds that are not unlike video game worlds and other sorts of virtual worlds. We have also seen that in our everyday lives we all act on the world like scientists. We act based on assumptions (hypotheses) and design our actions to elicit a certain sort of hoped for response from the world. If we want to survive, we pay close attention to the world's responses and design our new turns with due respect for these responses.

We have also seen that humans are capable of playing video games in their heads as ways to prepare for action and reflect on the results of action. This is not unlike scientists using models, simulations, and laboratories to save themselves from directly confronting the full complexity of the world unprepared.

We have also seen that when we talk (a form of action) or otherwise act, we act on the basis of a certain identity, body (skills, abilities), and tools. We have called this package of identity, body, and skills an "avatar". The avatar mediates our relationship with other people (who are complex worlds) and other sorts of worlds (real, artificial, virtual, augmented, and so forth). We seek for a good alignment between our effective abilities and affordances that we can use to accomplish our goals. We seek this good alignment in conversations with others, with the real world, and with games.

Alignment

The idea of aligning effective abilities with affordances via avatars in conversations with worlds (remember, people are worlds) is essential to success in life, not in terms of money, but in terms of living a satisfying worthwhile human life. There is a theory in genetics today with the provocative name "Experience Producing Drive (EPD) Theory" (Kaufman 2013). What this theory says is that we are each born with a unique set of genes. Every human wants to maximize his or her chance of survival. The genes we get control our motivations, inclinations, and preferences. As active agents we seek environments that maximize our survival. Different sorts of people seek out different sorts of environments, the ones in which they can flourish. We seek out environments where we can gain experiences that will allow us to gain the traits and skills we will need to live fruitful lives based on our own individuality.

As we seek experiences in environments where our motivations and preferences can flourish, those experiences develop our traits and skills. These traits and skills allow us to gain new more complex experiences in new more complex environments in which our traits and skills can develop further and get deeper. Genes lead to proactive attempts to find the right environments and experiences in which we can gain the traits and skills we need as unique individuals for a flourishing human life.

Note that even an initial small success can increment gradually into large-scale success. An initial "right fit" between person and environment gives rise to traits and skills that are just enough to take the next step in a new environment where the person will gain the skills necessary to go on to yet another step forward. We get "richer" bit by bit if we seek out a good fit between ourselves and the world.

This is why it is so crucial to help children to set a good trajectory early on. Positive nurturing for young children helps them find good initial environments where they can flourish and start the "bit by bit" process of improvement. Such nurturing also helps children learn to be proactive agents, searching out fruitful opportunities (for them) to learn, develop, and become healthy humans.

What happens to children that do not get such early help? Just as little initial successes prepare us for the next success until little "wins" add up to a "big win", so, too, initial losses can lead to being unprepared for the next experience. An initial little "loss" can lead to another and another until lots of little "losses" add up to a "big loss", a lost life. The poor get poorer. Worse, such children are in danger of not learning to be proactive agents on their own behalf, seeking out environments and experiences that align with their motivations, preferences, and developing traits and skills.

This incremental process of little wins leading to more until they amount to a big win and little losses leading to more until they amount to a big loss is called the "Matthew Principle" (from the gospel of Matthew: "For unto every one that hath shall be given, and he shall have abundance: but from him that hath not shall be taken even that which he hath", Matthew 25: 29), a process whereby the rich get richer and the poor get poorer (Stanovich 2000). Even a little initial loss means the child is less well prepared for the next learning opportunity. Even a little initial success means the child is better prepared for the next learning opportunity. And so on down the line of experiences and opportunities that constitute lives and careers.

EPD Theory (as I have developed it here) is a version of what we have been characterizing as the process of aligning effective abilities with affordances for actions that will accomplish goals. But there is one important addition here: EPD adds the idea that we need to be proactive agents in this search, considering our own unique motivations and preferences and developing traits and skills that are a good fit for us as a unique individual. And we all need help early on to get the process going by having some initial "little wins" and learning to be a confident proactive agent on behalf of our own learning, development, and success as a human, based on our own values and relationships with others and the world.

There is a proviso here that must be stated in an age where more and more we use digital media to customize and sometimes "dumb down" things for individuals. No one can fully know their strengths without accepting and seeking out challenges. Furthermore, often we discover some of our best skills and traits in collaboration with others. And, finally, often we find a true strength only after we have failed and tried again, perhaps a number of times.

Initial little wins are important, but so is learning to see failure as something we seek out and use as a tool for deep learning. It is just those people that have built up enough real confidence through good initial matches between their individuality and their environments that have the "grit" to persist past failure and even court failure. So, ironically perhaps, a string of little wins can build up not just to a big win, but also to the capacity to deal with failure in positive ways that lead to learning and development.

Conversations (with people and other worlds) are the process through which we humans align our effective abilities and affordances we can use. Since discourse analysis as we are developing it here is the study of such conversations, it is deeply involved with the nature of being human, with learning, development, and respecting ourselves and the world (or worlds) in which we live and hope to succeed.

Development

The connection to discourse and conversations will become clearer if we return to the notion of nurturing parenting above. What sort of early parenting (mentoring) gives rise to proactive agents, agents who actively seek the "right" environments and experiences on a life-long trajectory of human growth? A good deal of research suggests that such parenting involves the following things (Hart & Risley 1995; Tough 2012):

1 Lots of interactive talk between children and adults that involves talking about experiences and not just the "here and now" or direct orders.
2 Teaching children to negotiate in talk but with respect for others.
3 Teaching children to relate words to the world, to verbalize experience, and to relate texts to talk, other texts, and the world. Teaching children to make connections among all their experiences.
4 Allowing children the freedom to explore, take risks, and fail. This means lowering the cost of failure and teaching children that failure is a form of learning and development.
5 Letting children experience and play with the sorts of words, talk, ideas, values, and activities they will later see in school and the adult world.
6 Helping children develop "non-cognitive skills" like delayed gratification, the ability to persist past failure, and the desire to seek out and accept challenges. These are traits that are key to being a proactive agent. They correlate with school success better than IQ does.
7 Teaching children to respect evidence, others, and the world and use evidence proactively to learn, develop, and succeed.

All these features are key to good conversations with people and other worlds and they all develop through such conversations. It is important that children develop early on in life as proactive agents seeking out (with help) experiences for growth based on their own individuality as it exists in their genes and develops through experiences. It is important because of the process of little early "wins" incrementally leading through a trajectory of experiences (some of which will be failures) to a "big win", a good human life.

Nonetheless, a lack of opportunities to learn to be a proactive agent is something that can be remedied later if too much damage has not been done early on. It is remedied through the seven processes above, through nurturing mentoring from caring adults that leads to good conversations. However, we cannot take a short cut and skip the nurturing, mentorship, and small steps.

I have argued that discourse analysis can be a unified theory of conversations with other people and other sorts of worlds, conversations based on proactively aligning one's effective abilities with affordances for accomplishing goals. In that sense, discourse analysis is a theory of human life and development in the social, cultural, physical, biological, and institutional worlds with which we carry on conversations.

An example

Let me take a simple example. Below is the beginning of a conversation between a mother and her three-year-old child (data from Crowley & Jacobs 2002: 343–4). They have a plastic dinosaur egg and a little card that gives information about the egg:

> 1. Child: This looks like this is an **egg**.
> Mother: Ok well this …
> That's exactly what it is!
> How did you know?
> Child: Because it looks like it.
> Mother: That's what it says,
> see look *egg*,   *egg* …
> … Replica of a dinosaur *egg*.
> From the oviraptor.

This three-year-old is a little expert on dinosaurs (dinosaurs are for the child what Kevin Crowley calls "an island of expertise", see Crowley & Jacobs 2002). So we are in an area of alignment for the child in the sense that there is a very good fit between his interests, motivations, and inclinations and the environment. The mother is taking the opportunity to mentor the child into what will later be an avatar the child will "play" in school. She is displaying the identity, body, and tools of this avatar.

The child says that the plastic egg "looks like an egg". The child is speaking as an everyday person and as part of his early socialization in life. Normally, in everyday life, when someone says that something "looks like something", and it does, we just agree. The mother does just that, saying with excitement "That's exactly what it is!". It is a little win for the child.

Now the mother asks a question that could be seen as odd. She asks "How did you know?". Normally, in everyday life, when someone says something "looks like something" we do not ask such a question. The answer would be obvious: "Because I have seen eggs and know what an egg looks like".

Now the mother does something even odder. She points to the card—which the child is too young to read—and tells the child to see and look as she reads the word "egg" and then some of the other words on the card: "egg, egg … replica of a dinosaur egg. From the oviraptor". This seems odd, to tell a child who cannot read to look at print and then to read such "hard" (educated, book like, school-based) words to the child, words like "replica" and "oviraptor".

What is the mother doing? She is letting the child experience what will happen later in school when the child has to be a "student" (avatar) and "play school" (engage in a school Discourse). In school, though not always in the everyday world, we back up our claims not by what we have seen but by what we have read. Print is often a form of evidence or, at least, a source for answering teacher questions or tests. Words like "replica" and "oviraptor" are the sorts of "educated" book words students learn in school and eventually read in their school books. Such words are the way educated people talk about technical matters.

The mother has turned what could have been an everyday vernacular conversation into a technical conversation. She would not have done this save in an area where the child was a little expert and, thus, ready, inclined, and motivated to do so and learn in such an environment.

The child is learning how students talk, act, and value and what tools they have (e.g., print). The mother is preparing her child very early for one of the avatars in school and for game of schooling. The child now has another little win, a win in a game he cannot yet really play "for real". The way in which the mother scaffolds a win for the child in a game he cannot yet fully play is a form of working collaboratively within the child's "zone of proximal development" (the space where the child is ready to do with others what he will only later be able to do alone, see Vygotsky 1978).

Games

Well-designed games are good at working within players' zones of proximal development. They help the player find a good fit between motivations, preferences, and inclinations and environments in the game. They help the player develop X-ray vision to find alignments between effective abilities and affordances. They are good mentors, for players young and old.

Let's take as an example the game *State of Decay*, a game where the player has to live through a zombie invasion with other survivors who help each other. Figure 14.1 is a screenshot from the game.

FIGURE 14.1 Screenshot from *State of Decay*

State of Decay focuses on stealth, evasion, base building, securing resources, and combat. The game is in an open world and players' choices matter and can change the course of the game. Players build bases, watch towers, gardens, sleeping quarters, kitchens, workshops, medical bays, and libraries. There are multiple ways to solve the problems in the game.

Players start the game as Marcus, who is accompanied by his friend Ed. The opening of the game is, like so many others, a hidden tutorial where players discover what actions are available. In this opening, the player can explore at will, take time, practice and learn, without too much risk of failure.

When the player is ready, he or she moves on to the first base, where there are other survivors. Now the game starts "for real" as the player realizes that Marcus can die and if he does he stays dead forever. When he dies, the player can choose another avatar from among the other survivors. Each avatar has different skills and the player can level up each one in a number of different ways. If one set of choices has not worked well for the player, he or she can choose and develop the next avatar differently.

The player can experiment with different strategies and different choices, can retool mid game, and can readily learn from failure. I deeply regretted losing Marcus and re-started the game from the beginning to keep him alive. I could not do so. He died several times again, but by the last time, I finally really got how to develop an avatar and use the other survivors when my main avatar needed rest.

I realized all of sudden that I had gotten a lot better and had really learned to play and enjoy the game. Furthermore, it felt like I was doing it "my way" and that I had found a very good fit between my inclinations and skills and the game world. I was better and better at finding affordances I had the effective abilities to use well. I was able to choose a character from the survivors and develop her skills to fit with the way I wanted to play the game.

The game was encouraging me to be a proactive learner and searcher out of fruitful matches between my inclinations and skills and the environments and affordances in the game. It was allowing me to work in my zone of proximal development. It was giving good answers to the questions I asked it so long as I was prepared for failure and able to use it fruitfully. The game was not just a conversational partner, but a mentor.

Games play this mentorship role differently in different types of games. Different types of players find different types of games better fits with their preferred ways of learning. But nearly all games demand persistence past failure and proactive learning.

State of Decay is not preparing players for school or work in any direct way, though one could use similar design principles for other sorts of learning experiences designed for such purposes. Nonetheless, *State of Decay* allows gamers to play with exploration, search for good alignments, make and assess choices, and shape a world and accomplish goals through a conversation that respects the responses the game world gives back to players' probes (questions, actions). In that sense, it can be, like many other good games, a form of mindful playing with life and being.

However, I want to be clear that I do not consider that experiences are good just because they make us better at school or work. Experiences are good in and of themselves if they exercise us as proactive agents, humans caught up in the flow of enjoying challenges and gaining mastery.

The inventor of the modern IQ test—Alfred Binet—argued that what he called "direction", "adaptation", and "criticism" were the key components of intelligence (Kaufman 2013). Direction involves the ability to focus on a task and figure out what needs to be done. It has to do with managing attention well. Adaptation involves selecting appropriate strategies and monitoring and assessing their usefulness. This amounts, in part, to making good hypotheses and listening well to the world's responses. Criticism involves being able to criticize one's own thoughts and behaviors, and to make changes based on this criticism, changes that can improve performance. This means being able to reflect critically in and on our actions based on mental models or "video games" we run in our heads.

Managing attention, making and testing hypotheses, and reflecting well in and on action are core to good video game playing. Many well-designed games teach, encourage, and test such skills. In that sense, video games are a sort of pure play of intelligence. We should be clear, though, that Binet believed (unlike some of his latter day followers) that the skills of direction, adaptation, and criticism were teachable, learnable, and malleable, not fixed. Furthermore, modern research has shown that emotional and affective responses (i.e., caring) shape and direct how we use the skills that make up intelligence and are necessary to it.

Games place cognitive skills inside emotionally driven, highly motivating experiences where players care. This is what the mother was doing for her child and what we do for each other in our best conversations, discussions, and dialogues. It is what the world does for us, as well, if we treat it with respect.

The end

Well, that's all. I have attempted to develop a unified theory of discourse analysis that applies to talk, action, interaction, and games. It applies to life, learning, and development. It applies to writing and reading as "conversations in the head" that can lead to better conversations in and with the world, if done well.

We cannot yet really know whether this enterprise will or can work. This book is a first stab at something that has not been tried before. It may turn out to be a dead end or even a folly. But I hope that the book will be fodder for conversations in readers' heads and with each other that will be fruitful and fulfilling, even if I am wrong.

As I said in the last chapter, writers write out of an identity and address readers in terms of an identity. As a linguistic discourse analyst and a gamer and game researcher, I am attempting to write out of a hybrid identity that does not really exist, but which may someday exist. Many of you readers are not hybrid in this way, if you do not both game and investigate language, though you are hybrid in other ways. You have read as people interested in discourse, language, games, media, technology, or other things. I have invited you to imagine a way of reading that sees as belonging together things we have heretofore left apart (talk, games, worlds, science, development, and life as parts of discourse analysis). Thank goodness you can play video games in your head and imagine things that do not yet exist.

REFERENCES

Bakhtin, M. M. (1981). *The dialogic imagination*. Austin, TX: University of Texas Press.
——(1986). *Speech genres and other late essays*. Austin, TX: University of Texas Press.
Bikenstein & Malan (2008) *Basic theorycrafting*. Retrieved from: http://elitistjerks.com/f47/t20314-basic_theorycrafting/#ixzz0o13FOJlL.
Boethius (2009) Forum rules. Message posted to: http://elitistjerks.com/f74/a34-forum_rules_updated_1_28_09/#ixzz0piJUS2ig, 28 January.
Booth, W. C. (2005). "Resurrection of the implied author. Why bother?" In Phelan, J. & Rabinowitz, P., Eds., *A companion to narrative theory*. Oxford: Blackwell, pp. 75–88.
Chatman, S. (1978). *Story and discourse. Narrative structure in fiction and film*. Ithaca: Cornell University Press.
——(1990). *Coming to terms. The rhetoric of narrative in fiction and film*. Ithaca: Cornell University Press.
Crowley, K. & Jacobs, M. (2002). "Islands of expertise and the development of family scientific literacy". In Leinhardt, G., Crowley, K., & Knutson, K., Eds., *Learning conversations in museums*. Mahwah, NJ: Lawrence Erlbaum, pp. 333–56.
Duranti, A. (1997). *Linguistic anthropology*. Cambridge: Cambridge University Press.
Ferguson, C. H. (2012). *Predator nation: Corporate criminals, political corruption, and the hijacking of America*. New York: Crown.
Frank, R. H. (2011). *The Darwin economy: Liberty, competition, and the common good*. Princeton, NJ: Princeton University Press.
Frank, T. (2012). *Pity the billionaire: The hard-times swindle and the unlikely comeback of the right*. New York: Metropolitan Books.
Freire, P. (1995). *The pedagogy of the oppressed*. New York: Continuum.
Gee, J. P. (2004). *Situated language and learning: A critique of traditional schooling*. London: Routledge.
——(2007). *What video games have to teach us about learning and literacy*. Second Edition. New York: Palgrave/Macmillan.
——(2009). "Playing Metal Gear Solid 4 Well: Being a Good Snake". In Davidson, D., Ed., *Well Played 1.0: Video games, value and meaning*. Pittsburgh, PA: ECT Press, pp. 263–74.
——(2011). *Social linguistics and literacies: Ideology in discourses*. Fourth Edition. London: Taylor & Francis.

——(2013). *The anti-education era: Creating smarter students through digital learning*. New York: Palgrave/Macmillan.

——(2014a). *An introduction to discourse analysis: Theory and method*. Fourth Edition. London: Routledge.

——(2014b). *How to do discourse analysis: A toolkit*. Second Edition. London: Routledge.

——(2014c). *Good video games and good learning: Collected essays on video games, learning, and literacy*. Second Edition. New York: Peter Lang.

Gibson, J. J. (1979). *The ecological approach to visual perception*. Boston: Houghton Mifflin.

Goldfarb, W. (2003). *Deductive logic*. Cambridge, MA: Hackett.

Gould, S. J. (1980). *The panda's thumb: More reflections on natural history*. New York: Norton.

Hart, B. M. & Risley, T. R. (1995). *Meaningful differences in the everyday experience of young American children*. Baltimore: Paul H. Brookes.

Holland, D., Skinner, D., Lachicotte, W., & Cain, C. (1998). *Identity and agency in cultural worlds*. Cambridge, MA: Harvard University Press.

Hood, B. (2012). *The self illusion: How the social brain creates identity*. Oxford: Oxford University Press.

Howey, H. (2013). *Wool*. New York: Simon & Schuster.

Iser, W. (1974). *The implied reader: Patterns of communication in prose fiction from Bunyan to Beckett*. Baltimore, MD: Johns Hopkins Press.

Kahneman, D. (2011). *Thinking fast and slow*. New York: Farrar, Straus, & Giroux.

Kaufman, S. B. (2013). *Ungifted: Intelligence redefined*. New York: Basic Books.

Lampert, M. (2001). *Teaching problems and the problems in teaching*. New Haven, CT: Yale University Press.

Lampert, M., Rittenhouse, P. & Crumbaugh, C. (1996) "Agreeing to disagree: Developing sociable mathematical discourse". In Olson, D. & Torrance, N., Eds., *Handbook of education and human development*. Oxford, Blackwell's Press, pp. 731–64.

Lévi-Strauss, Claude (1968). *The savage mind*. Chicago: University of Chicago Press.

McDermott, R. (1993). "Acquisition of a child by a learning disability". In Chaiklin, S. & Lave, J., Eds., *Understanding practice*. London: Cambridge University Press, pp. 269–305.

Macknit, S. L. & Martinez-Conde, S. (2010). *Slights of mind: What the neuroscience of magic reveals about our everyday deceptions*. New York: Henry Holt.

Marr, D. (1982). *Vision: A computational investigation into the human representation and processing of visual information*. New York: Freeman & Co.

——(2010). *Vision: A computational investigation into the human representation and processing of visual information*. Cambridge, MA: MIT Press.

Morgan, V. M. (2010). *Emily Dickinson and hymn culture: Tradition and experience*. Surrey, England: Ashgate.

Mruczek, C. (2012). "Kiss your brain! Building the activity of leaning in schools". Arizona State Course paper (Discourse Analysis in Education).

Napier, S. L. (2005). *Anime from Akira to Howl's Moving Castle, Updated Edition: Experiencing contemporary Japanese animation*. New York: Palgrave/Macmillan.

Paul, C. (2011). "Optimizing play: How theorycraft changes gameplay and design". *Game Studies* 11.2, May. http://gamestudies.org/1102/articles/paul.

Pearson, P. D. (1997). "The first-grade studies: A personal reflection". *Reading Research Quarterly* 32.4: 428–32.

Sidnell, J. & Stivers, T., Eds. (2013). *The handbook of conversational analysis*. Oxford: Blackwell.

Smith, H. (2012). *Who stole the American dream?* New York: Random House.

Stanovich, Keith E. (2000). *Progress in understanding reading: Scientific foundations and new frontiers*. New York: Guilford Press.

Stiglitz, J. E. (2012). *The price of inequality: How today's divided society endangers our future*. New York: Norton.

Tough, P. (2012). *How children succeed: Grit, curiosity, and the hidden power of character*. New York: Houghton Mifflin.

Vygotsky, L. S. (1978). *Mind in society: The development of higher psychological processes.* Cambridge, MA: Harvard University Press.

Wright, J. (2008). "Self, video-games, and pedogogy". In Davidson, D., Ed., *Beyond fun: Serious games and media.* Pittsburgh, PA: ETC Press, pp. 127–35 (expanded version: http://thoughtmesh.net/publish/284.php#selfvideo, 2010).

INDEX

Lightning Source UK Ltd.
Milton Keynes UK
UKOW06f1808250816

281519UK00012B/256/P